AND THE
FORTUNE COOKIE

Takahiko Mukoyama
Tetsuo Takashima
with studio ET CETERA

GENTOSHA

PREVIOUSLY IN THE BIG FAT CAT SERIES

Ed Wishbone and his unfaithful pet cat
(忠実でない)
have finally managed to find
(find) (できる)
a new home and a new pie shop
— thanks to Professor Willy
and his homeless friends.

Now, Ed must help them back
by winning the prize money
of the State Pie Contest and
getting Professor Willy in a hospital.
But Willy is very sick and
there isn't much time...

"Yes."

"The contracts are signed. I want that street torn down by the end of next month. Yes, the one they call 'Ghost Avenue.'"

_{契約書} above "contracts"; _{引き裂く} above "torn"

"You did well with that shopping mall in Old Everville... Yes, that Out-something Mall. Wait."

Jeremy Lightfoot Senior pressed a button on the phone and switched lines.

"Yes? I see... All right. Good. Oh, and one more thing. If my son happens to win the contest, tell the judges he was responsible for Wishbone's problems."

"Yes. Disqualify him."

"Okay. How many pies now?"

The host stuck his head behind the curtain of the judges' booth and asked a staff member. The staff member was busy running around with pies in his hands. He shouted to the host.

"Sixteen. Almost done!"

"Okay. Time?"

"Thirty seconds and counting."

"Got it," the host said as he stepped back onto the stage.

"LADIES AND GENTLEMEN! Thirty more seconds! Most of the pies are finished, and the battle is coming to an end! This is Robert R. Silverman. Welcome back to the PIEGAMES!"

"Thirty seconds!?" George looked back at Ed. "Did he say thirty seconds?!"

"Don't stop! Keep going!" Ed shouted back to George, as he shook a saucepan full of blueberries. They were the only ones still baking. Most of the other contestants were cleaning up their booths. A lot of people in the audience were laughing and pointing at them.

"Twenty seconds!" the host announced.

Ed was covered with food — whipped cream on his head, flour spread over his shirt, and blueberry stains on his sleeves.

"Ten!"

The host cried, and the audience joined in.

"Nine!" they called out together.

Ed's hands were shaking badly. He tried to calm down but couldn't. The whole world seemed to spin around him.

"Ed! There's no time!" George cried out in panic.

Ed dashed to the table with his saucepan. But he moved too fast. He slipped and the saucepan flew through the air.

"Five!" the crowd counted.

Ed and George both tried to catch the saucepan. They both failed. The blueberries in the saucepan scattered all over the floor. Some of them splashed on Ed.

"Three!"

Ed and George stared at each other.

"Two!"

Ed closed his eyes.

"One!"

"BeeJees?"

Frank peeked at BeeJees to check if he was asleep. He was. Frank shrugged, and drove his wagon past BeeJees, whistling a tune from a cartoon show.

"Yaba daba daba... Yaba daba dooo..."

Willy had finally stopped shaking a while ago, and BeeJees had fallen asleep from exhaustion. Frank had come over to see if he was all right.

Something cracked beneath Frank's wagon. Frank bent down and found one of Willy's fortune cookies stuck under the front wheel. He reached down and picked it up.

The fortune paper was sticking out. He pulled it out and took a look.

"Mi... Mira..."

Frank tried to read it, but gave up. He laid the paper down gently beside Willy, and went back to the fire. Some friends of Willy's had gathered a pile of wood for them. Frank started adding wood to the fire.

Unnoticed by anyone, Willy's hand moved slightly. It touched the fortune paper Frank had set beside him.

The paper reflected the flickering red light of the campfire. Once, twice, it glowed. Then a gust of wind blew it into the fire, and it disappeared forever.

"Aaaand it's over!!"

The host raised his hand and announced aloud. Most of the contestants threw their hats and aprons up into the air and hugged each other. The audience applauded hard and the pie contest came to an end.

Ed was still holding the eggbeater in his hand. He had squeezed his eyes shut and was frozen in that position. George wanted to say something to Ed, but couldn't. All he could do was stare at the clock tower.

Two half-finished pies lay on the table. Ed and George sat silently on the floor as everyone else ran around them.

"Shucks," George licked the blueberry on his finger and mumbled to himself. "And it tastes so good too."

"Wishbone."

Ed looked up. It was Jeremy Lightfoot Jr. He had taken off his costume. He stood there staring at the unfinished pies. All around them, the contest staff was busy getting ready for the presentation of the pies.

Jeremy broke off a piece of Ed's unfinished pie, tasted it, and stared vacantly at the rest of the pie.

"Wishbone... About that *trouble* you had..."

Ed shook his head and got up. Purple syrup dripped from his shirt.

"It doesn't matter anymore," Ed said. "The contest's over."

He wiped blueberries off his forehead and started to walk past Jeremy. But Jeremy caught him by the arm.

"Listen, Wishbone. I need to tell you something."

Jeremy jerked Ed back. But before he could start talking, Jeremy saw the despair in Ed's eyes and closed his mouth.

"Ladies and gentlemen..." A voice from the speakers echoed above Ed's head. It was the owner of the New Mall. *"I think it's time to decide our winner."*

Ed silently took Jeremy's hand from his arm. He forced himself to smile.

"It's too late. This was the one time I couldn't fail... no matter what — but I did." Ed couldn't keep smiling any more, so he closed his eyes.

"It's over. Nothing can save us now."

Wrong.

"Holy Jesus Christ in heaven!!"

The owner almost had a heart attack as he took a look backstage. He staggered and almost fell, but somehow kept standing. He continued to stare at the incredible mess behind the curtains. It looked like a miniature hurricane had run through the pies.

After recovering from the first wave of shock, the owner realized he was still holding the microphone in his hand. He gulped, then spoke into it slowly.

"Um... Ladies and gentlemen, I'm... I'm really sorry. I think there's been... an *accident* backstage."

The owner could hear the audience stir as he said these words. He looked around the booth again. Almost all of the pies had been completely destroyed. He had no choice but to continue.

"Um... I'm sorry. We may have to cancel the contest."

The main tent had become a confused riot.

The owner and a few other staff members were trying to explain to the angry audience what had happened, but they were not succeeding. This was no surprise, because they had no idea themselves what had happened.

One staff member claimed he had seen "something like an incredibly fast bowling ball run out of the booth," but that was all they knew. The owner and the staff offered a rematch sometime next year, but that just made everyone angrier.

Ed, George, and Jeremy stood watching in silence as everyone fussed and shouted about the sudden developments. Ed took off his bandanna and stuck it in his pocket. He started to walk away.

"Where are you going, Wishbone?" Jeremy asked.

Ed didn't respond. He just walked out the back door. George and Jeremy stared at each other after the door closed.

In a corner near the judges' booth, the owner stood surrounded by angry contestants demanding a better answer. Everything was in chaos.

The contest is falling apart, Jeremy thought. *Just as Father would have wanted.*

In his mind, he heard his father laughing. Everything always seemed to end as his father had planned. He was sick and tired of it.

Jeremy walked over to the judges' booth, picked up a microphone, and switched it on.

"So why don't we do it now?"

Jeremy's voice boomed out of the speakers. Almost everyone stopped moving and talking. They all looked at Jeremy. Jeremy spoke through the microphone again.

"The rematch. Why don't we do it now?"

A long pause followed, and then one of the contestants shouted.

"Yeah, why not now?"

That was the cue. Everyone started agreeing all at once. The contestants began shouting for a rematch and the cries from the stands became even more fierce. George looked across the arena at Jeremy. Jeremy shrugged and laid down the microphone.

The owner was overwhelmed by the reaction of the crowd. He exchanged glances with the judges.

"Uh... Let us consider this for a moment, please."

The audience kept chanting "Rematch! Rematch!" over and over, louder and louder, until there was no other sound in the stadium.

"A rematch?"

Ed said to George with a bewildered look. He had been standing alone outside the main tent. George had come running over to him with the news. Ed asked again, "A rematch? Why?"

"The pies were all destroyed. They don't know why," George explained. "But everyone agreed on a second round. We're back in business, Ed!"

Ed had a look of pure surprise for a moment, but then he gradually lowered his eyes and nodded. George was almost dancing around, but he stopped when he noticed that Ed wasn't happy.

"What's the matter? We just got another chance, didn't we?"

"Yup," Ed said in a tired voice. "I know."

But he said nothing more. George looked worried.

"Are you okay? Want me to get you a cup of coffee or something?"

"Thanks. But no thanks," Ed said.

"What's wrong, man? Isn't this great news?"

Ed sighed and looked at George with a sad smile.

"George. You saw that pie we made. I was stupid to think we really had a chance to win."

George's usually happy face clouded over. Ed saw this and felt a tinge of guilt. He looked away.

"Even if I'd made the pie right, it was just a regular fruit pie. Nothing special. I'm sorry, George. You saw all those other pies. You know we don't have any chance of winning."

"But you *will* win," George said abruptly. "I know you'll win."

"George..." Ed said, hearing the sincerity in George's voice. George's trust in him was so genuine it scared him. "Thanks, but sorry. I... I'm really sorry."

Overhead, an announcement echoed from the speakers.

"... the PIEGAMES will restart at three o'clock, after a one hour break. During the break, contestants will be allowed to get extra supplies. We are very sorry for the inconvenience. If you choose not to watch the rematch, full refunds for your tickets will be..."

Ed looked away towards the Ferris wheel. George realized he was about to walk away, and tried desperately to say something to stop him — anything that would cheer him up, anything that would tell him how much George appreciated him. But this was too difficult for George. The truth was, he really believed that Ed would win. He just didn't know why.

"Ed!" George cried out helplessly.

"Your pies are the best!" he said. "The best in the world! *I know it!*" George kept shouting even after Ed had disappeared into the crowd. "Your pies are the best! I know it! I know it!"

The Ferris wheel was slowly rotating through the winter sky as Ed walked beneath it. He came to the far end of the carnival grounds and leaned on the outer fence. Hands in his pockets, he watched the Ferris wheel go around. His thoughts went around with it, around and around, almost as if he were hypnotized.

There are chances, and there are consequences.

The fortune cookie had said. He wondered whether the rematch was the chance or the consequence. He wondered if it even mattered.

You have no idea what a pie is made of.

Willy had said, but now he heard it in his own voice.

An endless stream of people walked past him. Some were families, some were couples, and some were alone. It was fascinating just to imagine all of the different lives, different problems, different feelings, and different tastes these people had.

It seemed crazy to make a pie that everyone would like. It was like finding a puzzle piece that fit every spot in the puzzle. It seemed impossible.

Ed spotted a balloon floating above the Ferris wheel. His mind wandered away with it.

Bake your pie.

Willy had said. He thought he was doing that, but now he wasn't so sure.

But I have responsibilities. I have to win.

But was that really true? Or was it just an excuse?

Your pies are the best.

George had said. And Ed had been ashamed. Because the pies he baked were really not his pies at all. He knew his pie was not as sour or sweet as a blueberry pie. It was different. It was different from anything else, and that was what frightened him — had frightened him, perhaps, for his entire life.

But he had found out that he was not the only one different. Willy was different. Frank was different. Everyone who lived on Ghost Avenue was different.

Ed closed his eyes. He thought about Jeremy and what he had said. He thought about George. And mostly, he thought about Willy.

Go, son. Bake your pie.

When he opened his eyes again, Ed was still looking up at the balloon in the sky. It was now high up in the clouds. The Ferris wheel continued its silent, slow movement.

You're going to be late again. You're going to fail.

The voice inside of him spoke again, but for the first time in his life, Ed ignored it.

The balloon had disappeared far off in the clouds.

It was time to bake his pie.

George was really getting worried when the clock read 2:55 and Ed still hadn't returned to the booth. All the contestants were already in place, ready to begin. George was about to go look for Ed when Ed burst through the back door and came running up to him.

"Sorry. I lost track of time. How's the oven?"

"Red-hot and ready to go," George said with a smile.

"Okay. Get everything out of that shopping bag," Ed said, pointing to a bag on the floor. "I'll get myself ready."

While Ed grabbed an apron and wrapped a bandanna around his head, George dug into the shopping bag. He stopped when he took out a yellow bottle.

"Uh... Ed!" George yelled in astonishment. "This isn't blueberry."

George showed Ed the bottle of mustard he held in his hand.

"I know," Ed replied in a confident voice.

"Oh..." George mumbled in a dumbfounded way and started placing the bottle on the table. But he turned around a second time. "No! Ed! You don't understand, man! There's a bottle of *mustard* in here!"

"George," Ed looked George straight in the eye and smiled. "I know."

George took a step back, fumbled with the bottle, and opened his mouth halfway.

"Uh-oh. You're not going to..."

Ed finished tying the bandanna on his head, rolled up his sleeves, and grabbed a cutting knife. It was one minute to three o'clock.

"I promised Willy I would go back and bake my pie. That's what I'm going to do," Ed said to George. "I'm going to bake *my* pie."

George saw a genuine smile come over Ed's face as he spoke. Ed seemed relaxed for the first time today. George still thought mustard pie wasn't a good idea, but he was happy that Ed was smiling again, and that was enough for George. He just nodded and put the mustard on the table.

And that was when the bell rang, and the battle of the pies began for the second and final time.

"Father! Just this once!" Jeremy shouted into the cell phone. "All I ask is... Father? Father!"

His father had hung up. Jeremy threw the cell phone at the wall of the trailer.

"Damn it!"

He stood up, grabbed the counter, and shoved it over. All the supplies on the table crashed to the floor. A few people in the audience noticed this and jumped in alarm.

"Boss? What happened? Boss!?" Jeremy's assistant cried out in surprise.

Jeremy ignored him and jumped down from the trailer. He meant to just walk straight out of the main tent. He was sick and tired of being himself, Jeremy Lightfoot Jr., son of the millionaire. He was just one step away from the back door when a voice called out to him.

"Jeremy!"

Jeremy stopped with his hands on the door. The voice came from the stands above him.

"Jeremy! Don't go! Jeremy!"

The voice cried out again. A very young voice. *Voices*, actually — because now his name was shouted from all over the stands above. Jeremy quietly looked up.

"Jeremy! You're the greatest!"

"Jeremy! Are you okay? Jeremy!"

Twenty or thirty children were crammed overhead in the stands, cheering and shouting. They had realized something was wrong, and had gathered above the Zombie Pies trailer. One of them started singing the Zombie Pies song and they all joined in.

" ♪ In the middle of the night, it's a heck of a fright! 'Cause the Zombie's in the kitchen and your stomach is all itchin'. So get out of that door, make your life a roar... Go to Zombie Pies! Go to Zombie Pies! ♪ "

Jeremy lowered his eyes, but the singing continued. He stayed that way, waiting for them to stop, but they kept on singing and singing.

"Ahhh, you meddling brats!" Jeremy still had his head down, but he spoke in a low, fiendish voice. When he raised his head, he had a pair of fake Dracula teeth in his mouth.

"You dare speak that way to the Zombie Lord!? The Zombie Lord is always triumphant!"

The kids cheered in delight. Jeremy gave a monster-like laugh and walked back up the stairs into the trailer. Once he was safely inside, he threw away the fake teeth and grabbed an apron. He shouted to his assistant.

"Forget everything. We're going to Plan B. I'm doing *Inferno*."

"Sir!?" Now the assistant was really upset. "But that pie is dangerous! You nearly burned yourself to death when you tried it in the lab!"

"I don't care. Get the marshmallows ready," Jeremy shouted as he spread flour on the surface of his counter. "I'll get the blowtorch from the truck."

But before he got started, Jeremy took a glance towards Ed, and then over at Billy Bob, who stood behind the trailer. Maybe he couldn't win at his father's game, but he still had his own way of playing.

And the game wasn't over yet.

"Okay, pie-lovers! I'm Robert R. Silverman! We're back again for the relaunch of the PIEGAMES! The television broadcast has already ended, so you folks here will be the only witnesses to the outcome today.

"It's five minutes past three and we're back on track with the rematch of the PIEGAMES! Two crowd favorites, Zombie Pies and Brown Butters are off to a quick start. Zombie Pies looks especially busy. They're using a giant mixer to beat something up.

"Meanwhile, across the stadium from Zombie Pies you'll find Ed Wishbone and his faithful partner 'the Tux'! Too bad they weren't able to complete their pies this morning.

"Well, what's this? Mr. Wishbone seems to have changed his recipe this time... and... oh my God, Ed! What the hell are you doing!?"

Ed poured a bottle of mustard into a hot saucepan right in front of the host. The mustard instantly bubbled and a sharp smell rose into the air.

"I'm sorry to tell you this, Ed, but I think you've made a terrible mistake." The host spoke to Ed with a sour face. "Oh man, *that* is not blueberry. It isn't even blue!"

Half of the audience laughed. The other half frowned as they smelled the burning odor of mustard. Ed ignored the banter and stayed focused on his saucepan. He grabbed a bottle of lemon juice and mixed in several spoonfuls of the liquid. The host seemed a bit irritated that Ed was not listening to him.

"Oh man, Ed! A *mustard* pie? I feel sorry for the judges."

Ed kept working. With quick movements, he added half a cup of honey, a few spices, and a bag of cottage cheese to the pan. Then he tossed in a big bowl of graham crackers that George had crushed, and stirred the entire mixture with a large wooden spoon.

"Uhhm... that looks almost like food if you..." That was the moment a rich spicy aroma rose up out of the saucepan and reached the host's nose. The host's high-speed patter slowed down for the first time today as he inhaled the sweet and sour smell of Ed's recipe.

Some of the laughter from the audience also died down. They finally noticed the serious, determined look on Ed's face. Ed threw a splash of red wine into the pan. The wine caught fire and burned high for a moment. The mouth-watering smell grew even richer in the air. Suddenly, the barrel oven, the mustard, and the tuxedo weren't as funny as before.

"George! The crust!" Ed shouted to George as the audience watched.

George dashed to the oven. He took out a beautiful golden-brown crust from inside. It too gave off a slight smell of mustard. Spicy, but sweet. The host cleared his throat and spoke in a somewhat lowered tone.

"Well, okay. Let's see how the other contestants are doing. Here in the next booth, we have the famous Buffi Brothers..."

The host started walking away to the next booth, but couldn't help glancing back at Ed. The smell was growing richer and richer, filling the whole stadium now.

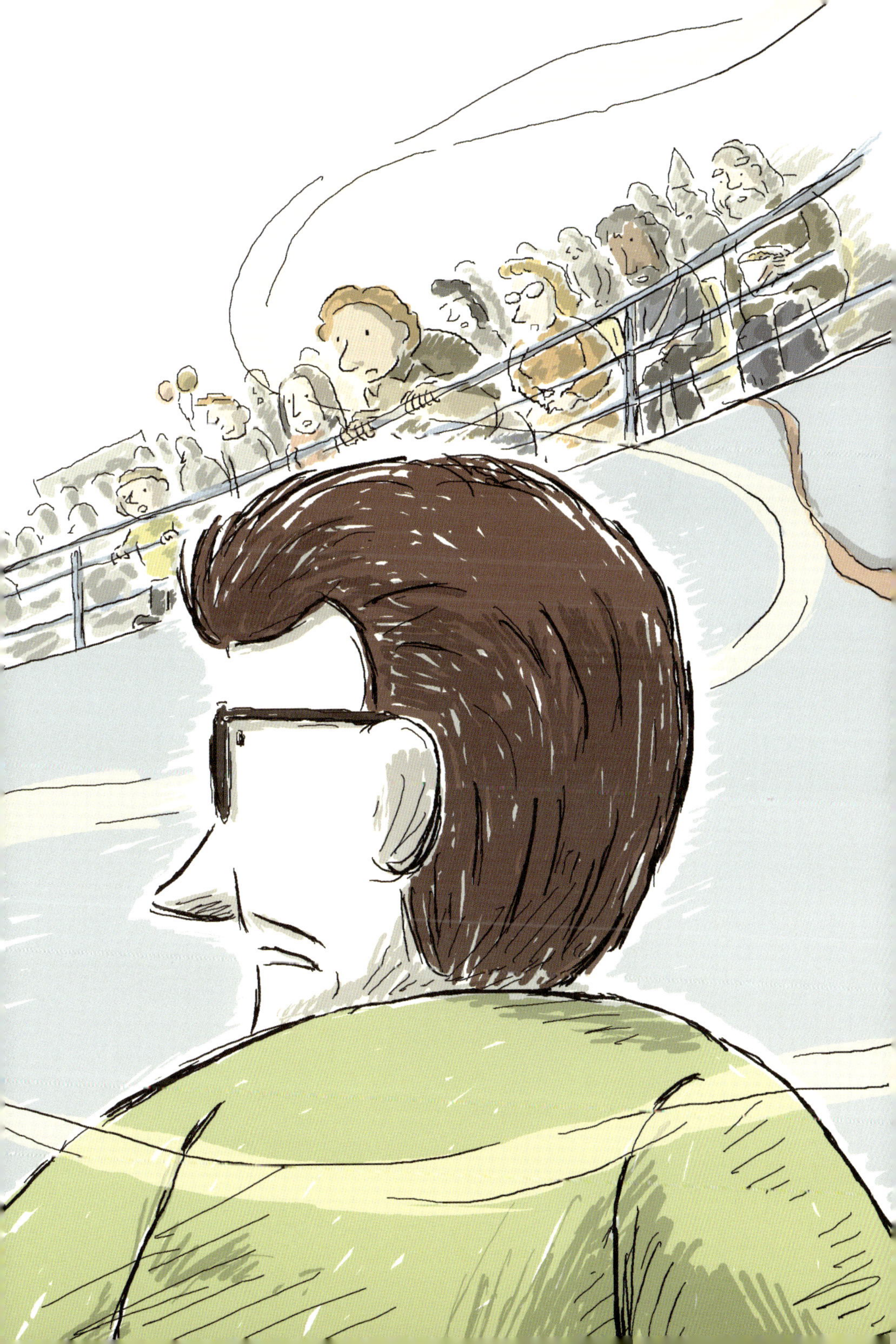

"George! How are the pies?"

"Looking good! Give them another five minutes."

"Gotcha," Ed said, and George smiled.

"Anything else?" George asked.

"Nope. Now we wait."

It had been a fast, yet incredibly long, hour and a half. Ed was finally able to relax and take a deep breath. That was when he saw something walk past the back door. It made him freeze.

"Cat?" Ed rubbed his eyes. "No. Can't be..."

Ed walked slowly to the back door and peered down the alley. There was no sign of anything. He was half convinced it had just been his imagination. But a number of boxes and crates were lined up along the wall, and there were plenty of hiding spaces for a cat.

"Ed, where you goin'?" George asked with a worried look as Ed took a step out the back door.

"Nowhere... Just getting some fresh air," he answered.

"Come back soon, man! The pie's almost finished."

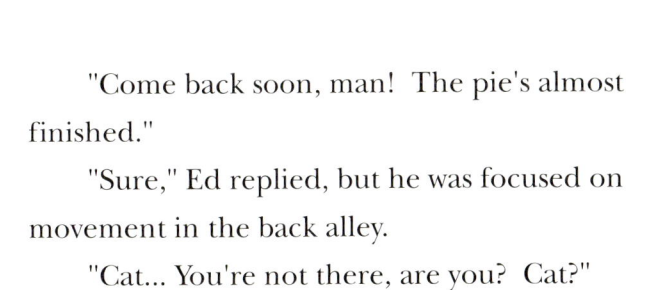

"Sure," Ed replied, but he was focused on movement in the back alley.

"Cat... You're not there, are you? Cat?"

Ed whispered as he walked past a pile of boxes. Nothing was there but some trash. He reached the end of the alley and opened the emergency exit to look outside. There was only an empty field beyond it. He sighed with relief.

At that exact moment, Billy Bob stepped out from behind Ed and grabbed him by the neck. In a moment of panic, Ed tried to loosen Billy Bob's grip, but Billy Bob was much, much stronger.

"Give up. Quit the game. *Now*," Billy Bob whispered.

Ed kept clawing at Billy Bob's hands. But it was no use. He choked and gasped as Billy Bob tightened his grip further. Ed's face was starting to turn blue.

"Stop! Goddammit! Stop! You're going to kill him!"

Someone hit Billy Bob in the back with a gasoline can. Billy Bob grabbed the intruder and slammed him against the boxes near Ed. There was a mild expression of surprise on his face when he saw that it was his boss's son.

Jeremy scrambled to his knees and shouted at Billy Bob.

"You stop this right now or I'll call the police."

Billy Bob ignored Jeremy and turned to Ed again.

"I'm not going to quit," Ed said abruptly. His legs were shaking badly with fear, and he was almost in tears, but he went on anyway. "They're waiting for me back on Ghost Avenue. I can't quit."

Ed was trying really hard to stand up straight, but his thin, weak legs refused to hold him up. Billy Bob didn't hesitate. He moved towards Ed. Only moments before Billy Bob's hands reached Ed, a low purr came from the ground below.

All three looked down.

Mr. Jones had finally found its way back and was brushing its side against Jeremy's leg. It went over to Billy Bob and started rolling around on his shoes, purring all the while.

Billy Bob watched this through his dark sunglasses. The two pie bakers continued to huddle on the ground while the cat went on rolling. A long, awkward moment passed. Billy Bob shook his head.

"You," he said to Ed. "You need more spice."

Ed kept quiet, not knowing what to say. He was still recovering his breath. He didn't know whether Billy Bob was referring to him or his pie. Billy Bob turned to Jeremy.

"And you. It's Ms.! Not Mr.! Next time, *check*, you stupid brat!"

Having said that, Billy Bob took a long breath. He looked at the bewildered faces of the two, shook his head again, and walked off without another word. Ed and Jeremy stared at each other.

"What... what was that all about?" Jeremy murmured.
_{ぼ そ っ と 言 う}

"I have no..."

Ed suddenly remembered the time and grabbed Jeremy's arm. He took a quick look at Jeremy's watch. He gasped, and hurried to his feet. Still shaking, he ran back to his booth on weak legs.

Left alone with Mr. Jones, Jeremy sat there for a while, mumbling something to himself. Then, suddenly — he understood what Billy Bob had said.

Jeremy grabbed Mr. Jones and raised the cat up in the air. Mr. Jones relaxed and purred.

A moment later, Jeremy's eyes opened wide with surprise.

Fifteen more minutes.

George had to make a choice.

The rims of the pie were already a bit too brown. In a few seconds, it would be too late. Ed had not come back and it was up to him to rescue the pies.

He was scared to do anything, but he knew in his heart that if he didn't get the pies out now, they would burn. So he took a deep breath, prayed that he was doing what was right, and pulled out the two pies.

As George was laying the two pies on the table, a wheezy Ed came tumbling into the booth behind him.

"George, are the pies okay?"

"Ed! God! I was so worried, man! I didn't know what to do!"

Ed looked at the pies on the table and sighed with relief.

"George. Thanks. You were great. Now, c'mon, let's finish. We only have ten more minutes."

"Gotcha!" George replied and handed Ed the decorations they had made from sugar and marzipan. Ed was about to place the first one on the pie when he suddenly stopped.

"Something wrong?" George asked.

"No," Ed said. "It's just..."

The pie was beautiful the way it was. It had only a simple golden-yellow surface, but the color was beautiful. Ed hesitated. He looked around the arena at the other booths.

Most of the pies were finished. They were all decorated with splendid colors, looking more like works of art than food. The whole arena was also much like the pies. All colorful, glamorous, and wonderful.

But as he stood there looking around, it all suddenly seemed strange to Ed. For a few seconds, all of the sound and racket faded into the distance, and Ed could see for the first time—

without any distraction — the whole scene of the contest before him. And it seemed strange. It seemed like he was lost in a world he didn't know.

He remembered his mother's pie. So simple, so beautiful.

He remembered the fake apple pie he had made that first morning on Ghost Avenue. It was simple too. Maybe not beautiful, but simple and warm.

Ed quietly put the decorations back down. He said to George,

"Let's leave it this way."

George gasped.

"Why?! Ed! Are you out of your mind? Look at all the other pies, man!"

Ed smiled. "This is our pie. It has to be simple."

George was dumbfounded for a moment, but he looked at the decorations, then at Ed, then at the barrel oven, and then finally, at himself.

"I... I guess you're right," George said. "There ain't (aren't) no decorations on Ghost Avenue, you know."

That made them both smile. Ed added a simple ring of yellow whipped cream around the rims of the pies, then handed the two pies to George. George went running to the judges' booth.

Jeremy walked out of the Zombie Pies trailer almost at the same time. His assistant was rolling a giant carrier (運搬台). Ed and Jeremy's eyes met across the arena.

A few minutes later, the bell rang for the second time, and the PIEGAMES were officially (公式に) over.

"Good evening! This is Glen Hamperton reporting for the evening news. We're back at the state pie festival! Hundreds have called us insisting that we follow up on the rematch of the contest... Well, here we are with a special live report, just in time for the finale.

"The baking is all finished. The contestants are now presenting their pies to the audience. The local Chinese favorite, 'Sugar & Spice,' has just finished their mystic oriental dragon dance... and now Goo Goo Planet is up on stage. Something like a flying saucer is landing in the middle of the stage.

"Uhm... too bad. The audience doesn't like them too much. Frankly, I don't blame them. Thank God... it seems to be over now.

"Only a few contestants seem to be left, and... oh-oh, a weird drum beat has just started up in the arena... Is that...

"Yes! It is! Ladies and gentlemen, you're all in luck, because we're just in time for the big show! Here they come! Get ready!
"ZOMBIE PIES!!"

A cloud of red smoke began to fill the arena as a low beating of drums sounded inside the tent. The smoke suddenly parted in the middle, and Jeremy appeared from within the cloud.

The Gravedigger followed behind him, carrying a huge tray with a blue velvet cloth spread over it. Red spotlights from the top of the Zombie Pies trailer flew around Jeremy as the volume of the music stepped up.

"Behold!! The fiery gates of the Inferno!"

Jeremy shouted and drew the velvet cloth from the tray. A huge pie that resembled a red forest in a snow-covered land appeared from under the cloth.

Jeremy raised his hand and the music suddenly stopped. The Gravedigger placed the tray on a stand and hurried away.

The audience fell silent, staring at Jeremy and his pie. After standing absolutely still for a moment, Jeremy waved his hand at the pie. A giant blaze of fire burst out from under his cape. It covered the surface of the pie in flames for a few seconds, then disappeared as suddenly as it had appeared. After the fire, the soft, marshmallow-white surface of the pie had been toasted a delicious golden-brown. The forest had melted into a spectacular mound of red toffee.

The crowd applauded intensely as Jeremy took a bow.

Meanwhile, behind the stage.

"Ed. You all right, man?"

"I don't know."

"You're up next."

Ed nodded. George looked around the stands surrounding them, and said in a weak voice.

"Man, I'd be scared if I was you."

"George, I *am* scared," Ed assured him.

"Ed Wishbone, will you please come to the stage!" The voice from the speakers called his name.

"That's you," George said.

Ed just nodded again and started walking towards the stage. His legs were stiff as sticks. On the last moment, George remembered to hand Ed something. Ed took it and opened his hand. Willy's fortune cookie lay in his palm. Ed took a deep breath, and managed a smile.

"Thanks, George. I'll try my best."

Jeremy was just coming down from the stage. Ed and Jeremy's eyes met as they passed each other.

"Your turn," Jeremy said. It was only a whisper. He was holding his right hand inside his cape. Ed noticed it was burned pretty badly. Jeremy's assistant came rushing up to him with a bucket of ice water as soon as Jeremy sat down. Jeremy dipped his hand in the bucket and grunted with pain.

"Ed Wishbone? Are you there?"

The announcer called out again. Ed walked out onto the stage. A spotlight came searching for him.

As the spotlight guided him to the center of the stage, Ed was surprised to hear a lot of clapping coming from the audience. He saw a microphone waiting for him. His pies were there too, displayed on a table. He walked forward, but very stiffly.

When he reached the microphone, Ed took a breath and looked around the arena. Hundreds, maybe thousands of eyes fell on him. He swallowed.

He tried to say something, but his mind was completely blank. He tried to think of something to say, anything, but his brain simply refused to work.

"Hello."

He said finally, his voice trembling a little. A few people in the audience laughed.

"I'm Ed Wishbone. I used to own a pie shop. But now, I live down on Ghost Avenue."

A stir went through the crowd.

"A lot of people live there — and they're all kind to me. They... they are poor. Really poor. It's certainly not the best place to live, but it's... it's still my home. It's the only home I have."

As he spoke, Ed felt the warmth of the campfire in the cinema. The peaceful night sky above Ghost Avenue spread through him. He opened his hands and was surprised that the sweat on his palms had dried. He felt a little calmer than before.

"These past weeks have been a very hard time for me... But somehow, it all seems a lot more precious than the rest of my life. Weeks that I'll never forget."

A quiet rush of memories flew through Ed's mind as he said these words. Losing his shop, running to the bank, waking up in a ghost town... everything seemed like such a long time ago. Ed took a long, deep breath, and continued.

"Sometimes... I think the best pie isn't always sweet. Sometimes it's not sour or bitter either. Sometimes... I think... I think that it can even be a mustard pie."

Ed lowered his eyes to his pie. And for a second, the words Billy Bob had said to him came back as an echo.

Spice. You need more spice.

"It's a little spicy at first, but we all need some spice to recognize the sweetness hidden underneath. I've learned in these past few weeks that a good pie is a lot like real life. Everyone's life.

I used to spend a lot of time leaning on the counter of my old pie shop, wondering why no one came to buy my pies. But I think I know now."

The audience had become almost completely silent. Ed was so absorbed in his thoughts that he didn't notice.

"I tried so hard to make good pies... great pies, but being a baker, a pie baker, isn't really about making pies..." Ed took another deep breath, and said in a firm voice, "it's about making people happy."

The audience remained silent. Ed had expected laughter, so he felt relieved as he whispered into the microphone.

"Uh... That's all. Thank you for listening. Thank you."

The applause that came a moment later was big. Really big. And the applause continued — for a long, long time.

The cat walked down the center of the fairgrounds gracefully, almost dragging its full tummy on the ground. It suddenly came to a stop when Ed stepped out of the main tent, his bandanna in one hand and an exhausted look on his face. Ed spotted the cat immediately, but didn't seem surprised.

"I thought I saw you," Ed said to the cat.

The cat cautiously retreated a few steps.

"Don't worry, the contest's almost over. I'm not going to try and catch you and get my only good shirt ripped."

Ed sat down on a bench near the cat. The cat frowned, but decided Ed was not a concern.

Ed watched the glimmering lights of the carnival in silence, with the cat at his feet. The applause was still echoing back inside the arena, but it all seemed far away. The glamour, the importance, and the meaning of the contest felt vague to Ed as he sat there.

Ed looked at the cat. Their eyes met for a moment.

"I used to have a fairly peaceful life, you know," Ed said softly. "Until that day you came into my shop. Since then, my life has been one big roller-coaster ride. No thanks to you."

The cat seemed not to care. It just yawned and continued licking its paws.

"But you know what, cat?" Ed said. "I think I'm starting to like roller coasters."

A low purr echoed a few feet away. Ed looked up. He saw Jeremy sneaking out of the tent with a cat cage in one hand. Jeremy had his heavy coat on, and seemed to be leaving.

"Damn," Jeremy said. "Why are you out here?"

Ed shrugged. "What about you?"

Jeremy's cat purred again in its cage. The Big Fat Cat opened one eye, took a look, and then closed it.

"I'm going home," Jeremy said.

"Why? What about the results?"

Jeremy sighed.

"I'm smart enough to know when I've lost. I just don't want to see the kids when they find out. And your pie..."

Jeremy realized he was talking too much. He coughed, and went on more slowly.

"... Uh, nothing. Well, anyway, it's okay. I really don't need the prize money, you know." He shrugged. "I'm rich."

"Ed!"

Just then, George flew out of the main tent, a look of awe on his face. He was trying to say something, but the words seemed to be stuck in his mouth.

"George." Ed rose, worried that something had happened again. "Is everything okay? Did the judges reach a decision?"

George smiled, and with tears forming in his eyes, said in a warm voice.

"Oh yeah. Yeah, they sure did."

Jeremy shrugged as he watched Ed and George run back into the main tent, back into the growing applause. He said to The Cat Formerly Known As Mr. Jones,

"Don't worry. I'm okay." Jeremy patted the cat's cage. "C'mon, let's go home."

Jeremy slowly walked away into the night, whistling the theme music of Zombie Pies.

"Willy! BeeJees! Frank! We're back! We've got the money!"

Ed called out as he entered the cinema. George was one step behind him. The cinema lobby was almost completely dark. Ed and George hurried through the piles of junk.

"C'mon! There's a taxi waiting outside! I already called the hospital!"

Ed shouted louder as he approached the swinging doors.

"I'm sorry I'm late! We had an accident and..."

Ed pushed the doors open and stopped short. The hall was silent. His voice echoed in the empty space.

"Willy?"

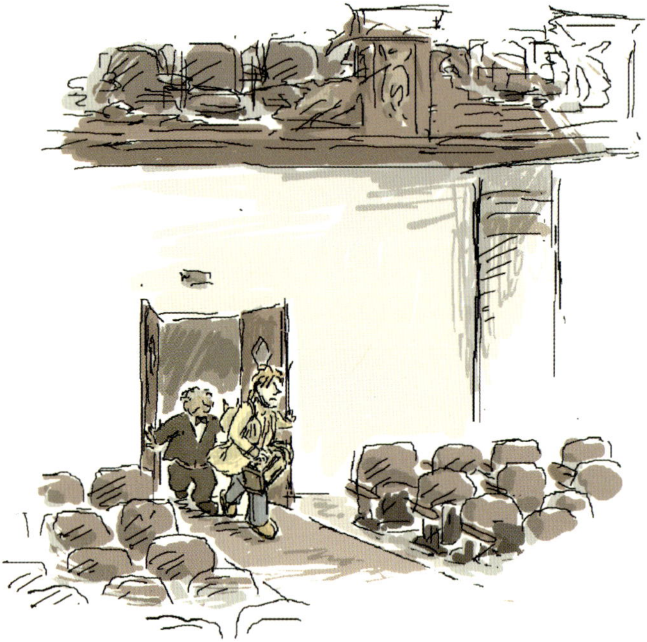

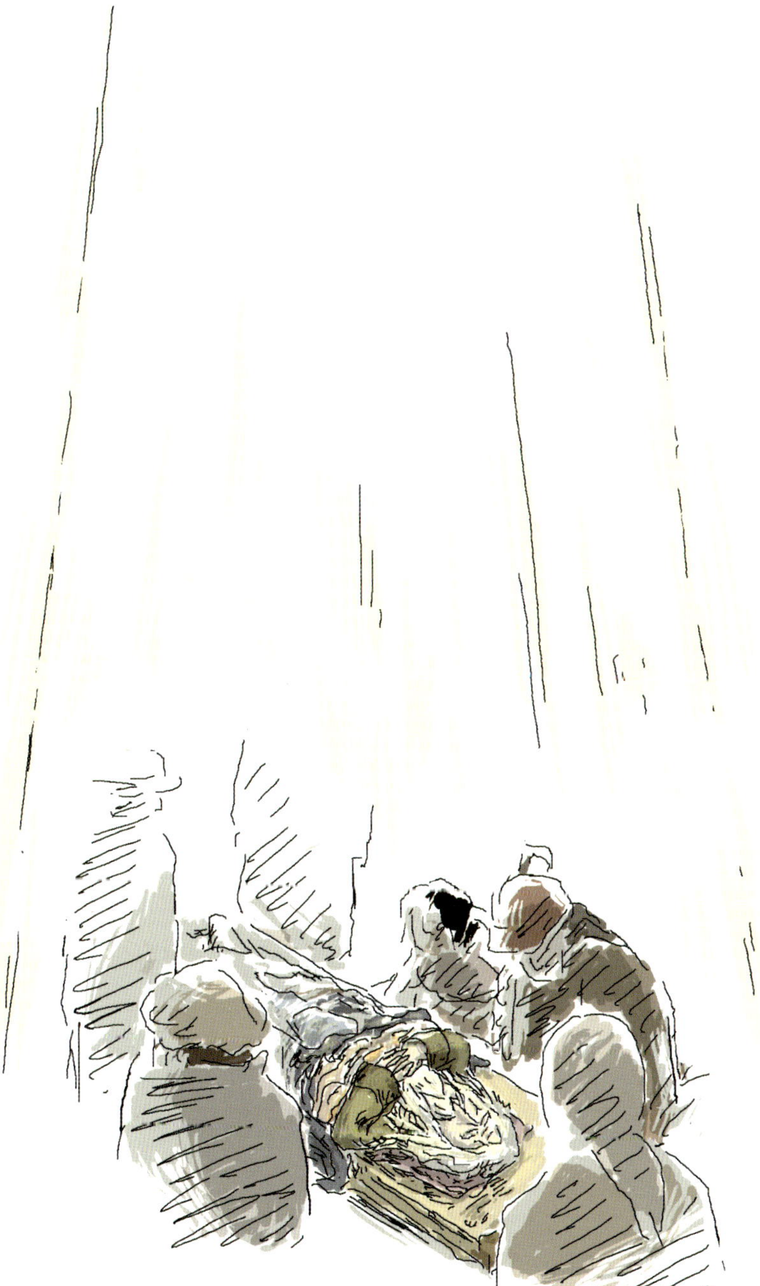

The cinema was absolutely silent. Step by step, Ed slowly approached Willy.

Willy was completely still. Not only Willy, but the air around him also seemed still. Time itself seemed still there. Ed knew that Willy was dead.

"It was about an hour ago," BeeJees said. He held his face in his hands, squatting against the ragged bed.

"He suddenly opened his eyes and smiled. I thought maybe he was waking up and I ran over to him. He was already dead."

"Wh... why..."

But Ed couldn't continue. The words remained in his mouth. He tried to swallow, but his mouth was dry. Willy wore a smile on his face. He looked like he was proud of something.

"I think he knew," BeeJees said as he laid his eyes on the trophy in Ed's hands. Tears gleamed in his eyes. "I think he knew."

Ed closed his eyes tight. He was trembling slightly.

The light of the moon was a soft tender yellow against the darkness of the world. It shined on Willy as if it were guiding him to a better world. A world without hunger or pain or cold. A world where he could finally rest. A world that was not cruel like the one they had to live in.

"I don't know how... But I..." BeeJees broke down as he spoke. "I... really think he knew... and I think... I think he was happy."

The Golden Crust trophy glittered in the moonlight as it fell from Ed's hands, rolled on the floor, and lay still in the dark.

The silence of the night slowly eased the tension of the long hard day. The temperature was almost below zero. Ed's breath turned white as he walked down the dark street, the Golden Crust trophy in his hands. He chose a place on the sidewalk, and sat looking up at the stars. He watched them for a long time, as if he could find Willy among them — if he looked hard enough.

Behind Ed, the cat played around with the Golden Crust trophy. The cat had realized it wasn't a real pie some time ago, but it kept playing anyway.

All the excitement of the day seemed like a dream far away as Ed sat there in the cold. He remembered the day he met Willy, right there on the street. He remembered his soft voice. He remembered his careful words. And most of all, he remembered his soothing smile.

"What am I going to do now, Willy?" Ed whispered into the empty space around him. The words turned white and disappeared immediately. "What, Willy? *What?*"

After a long pause, Ed took the fortune cookie out of his pocket. He stared at it for a moment, then cracked it open. A thin piece of paper was inside. Ed read it.

Most treasures are in the places you first find them.

Ed read it over and over again, trying to find some meaning in the words. Some answer. But only tears came and fell. He cuddled his knees and cried. The cat just continued to play with the trophy.

Up above town, the first flakes of snow started to fall, announcing the arrival of a long, cold season. A church bell rang far away in the mountains. The snow quickly grew stronger, and soon, the town of Everville was covered with the color of winter.

December 25th.
It was Christmas Day.

NEXT: One last story.

BFC BOOKS PRESENTS:
洋書の世界の歩き方

そろそろ洋書の世界へ旅立つ時。
リュックに入れるのはたったひとつ、想像力だけ。
BFC が贈る、初心者のための洋書ガイド。

PROLOGUE
〜 本を探す 〜

　みなさまの応援のおかげでここまで来ることができた **BFC BOOKS** も、ついに残すところ一冊となりました。猫とエドの旅が行き着く先がどこなのか、その答えもまもなく出ようとしています。このシリーズはその時、ひとつの終わりを迎えますが、英語の楽しさを学ぶ旅はまだまだ続きます。

　世界には面白い本がたくさんあります。もしこのシリーズをここまで読んできた方なら（とばしとばしだってかまいません）、もう世界中の英語の本を読み始める準備はできています。まだ読み始めていないとしたら、そろそろ広い洋書の世界へ踏み出す時です。

　といっても、何から読んだらいいのか分からない、読みたい本が見つからないという方もいることでしょう。そんな方にぜひおすすめしたいのが欧米の児童書です。

　決して簡単だからではありません。一般書に比べて読みやすいのは確かですが、それはおまけの理由に過ぎません。児童書を読んでほしいのは、児童書が最高に楽しい本のジャンルだからです。

　アメリカの一般家庭の本棚には、たいていたくさんの児童書が並んでいます。子供が読むためだけではありません。大人が大事に並べています。——なぜそんなにみんな児童書が好きなのか、まずはその秘密に迫りながら、シリーズ最後の長編解説となる今回は、じっくりと「児童書の世界」をご案内させてください。

Jeremy Lightfoot Jr.'s
Words of Wisdom

"Time is money.
But the exchange rate is low."

> アメリカの読書事情

　アメリカは児童書の天国のような国です。
　大人でも夢中でページをめくるような面白い物語から、美術館に入るような絵本まで、素晴らしい本がたくさんあります。その上、カラフルに装飾された子供図書館（**Children's Library**）がどこの町にもあって、そこでは本が借り放題になっています。また、映像資料や音読本なども充実しているほか、季節ごとに「読書グランプリ」が開催され、子供たちは一カ月間に読んだ本の数を競い合います。大会で優勝すると豪華な賞品がもらえるので、子供たちも本気で取り組み、優勝する子は一カ月に 100 冊以上の本を読んでいることも珍しくありません。

　意外に知られていないことですが、アメリカは教育の過程で「読書」をとても重要視しています。各小学校にはたいてい充実した図書室（大きな学校だと図書館）があって、何かにつけては「図書室に行って調べてくるように」と先生に言いつけられるので、分からないことがあったら図書館へ行くという習慣が身につきます。
　読書の宿題もよく出ます。しかし、問答無用で「読め」というものではありません。カラフルなイラストに彩られた本のリストを渡されて、子供が自分で好きな本を選びます。そのリストは必ずしも「名作」や「良書」と言われるような作品ばかりではなく、「子供にとって本当に面白い本」を中心に選ばれています。

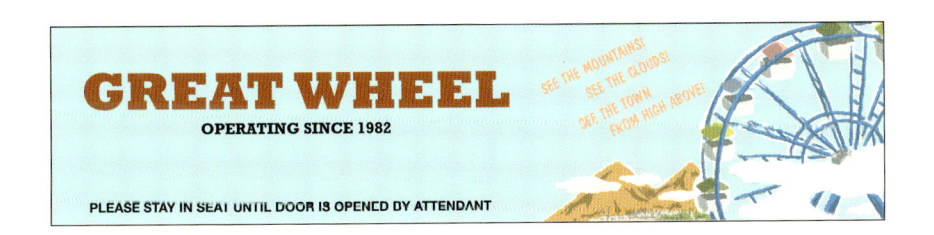

最初に読んだ本がつまらなかったら、その子が一生読書を嫌いになる──アメリカの大人たちはそれをよく知っているので、このリストを作る時は本当に真剣に、慎重に一冊一冊を吟味しています。だからこそどの本を選んでも、子供たちは本と過ごす魔法の時間を味わうことができます。

　ここにちょっと意地っぱりなアメリカ人の少年がいます。彼が小学校で初めて本を読む経験を通して、アメリカの人々が本を好きになっていく過程を一緒に感じてみてください。

A KID AND HIS BOOK

① 先生から本のリストをもらう

② 仕方なくかっこいい表紙の本を選ぶ

③ しばらくほっておく

④ 退屈なので昼休みに数ページだけ読んでみる

⑤ なんとなく続きが気になる

⑥ 学校帰りに体育館の裏の階段に腰かけて読み始める

A CAT'S ~~TAIL~~ TALE

Big Fat Cat and the Fortune Cookie

⑦ 読み続ける

⑧ 読み続ける

⑨ 読み終わる（帰りが遅くて怒られる）

⑩ ちらちら読み返してみたりする

⑪ 何か読む物がないと落ち着かなくなる

⑫ 以下、想像にお任せします

⑬ そして……三十年後

⑭ 歴史は繰り返す

⑮ ずっと……

　多くのアメリカ人はこんな感じで本を好きになっていきます。一冊のペーパーバックをぼろぼろになるまで読んで、映画化されたら最前列で観て、そして、自分が親になった時には、今度はその本を子供に買い与えます。表紙が変わって、新版になったその本を子供よりも先に読み返して、「やっぱり面白い！」と思いながら。

Not so long ago...

自分だけの「ベスト100冊」

　ここまで読書を大切にする環境は、残念ながら今の日本にはありません。子供は児童書よりも漫画に夢中です。漫画の方が面白いのだから無理もありません。アメリカで子供が児童書を読むのは、単純に児童書が漫画に匹敵するほど面白いからです。

　本に慣れ親しんで育った欧米人の多くは、大人になって一般書に進んだあとも、児童書を読み返すことがよくあります。好きなシリーズをその後、何十年も買っている人も少なくありません。それは児童書というジャンルが一般書の下位に位置するものではなく、一般書と同等、あるいはそれ以上の力を持った作品にあふれているからです。そして、もちろん面白さには大人用も子供用もありません。

　だからこそ、大人になってから自分の「ベスト100冊」をあげろと言われれば、本好きのアメリカ人のリストには、得てして何冊かの児童書が入ります。これは大人の本を無数に読んだあとでさえ、決して色あせない物語がたくさんあることを意味しています。もしそんな一冊に出会うことができたら、きっともっと英語を好きになれるのではないでしょうか。

　もちろん、すべての児童書の中からいい本を探し出すのはたやすいことではありません。しかも、日本人がそれに挑戦する場合、「面白さ」と、英語としての「難易度」のバランスをとるのが至難の業です。例外もありますが、一般的には難易度が上がるほど表現力も上がるので、ある程度難しい本の方が、より複雑で味わい深い物語である可能性が高いのは確かです。しかし、だからといって、最初から難易度の高い本に挑戦すると、「面白さ」を感じる前に疲れてしまうこともよくあります。

　自分に適正な難易度は「あまり辞書を使わなくても、イライラせずに読める本」です。しかし、読めたとしても、面白くなければ、やはり最終的には挫折してしまいます。楽しく読めるレベル内で、最高に面白い本を見つけること――これは確かに簡単なことで

There was a box full of kittens on the side of a road.

はありません。

　今回はそんな探索の手助けとなる、おすすめの本のリストを作りました。といっても、最初に紹介するのはたったの三冊。「基本の三冊」となる三つの作品です。どれも『ビッグ・ファット・キャットとフォーチュン・クッキー』とほぼ同じぐらいの難易度で、雰囲気や内容も **BFC** シリーズと似た手触りの本ばかりです。読む時のサポートとなる挿絵もたくさん入っています。

　まず、この「基本の三冊」を通して、洋書の世界を歩き始めてください。

Two were white, two were striped, and two had spots on their back.

STEP 1
〜 本を選ぶ 〜

「基本の三冊」のうち、まず最初に紹介するのはたくさんの楽しいお菓子に彩られた傑作ファンタジー『Charlie and the Chocolate Factory』です。

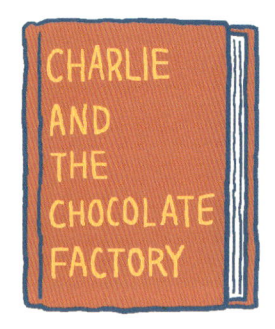

Charlie and the Chocolate Factory by Roald Dahl
　この物語の主人公チャーリーは、寝たきりのおじいさん・おばあさんを二組抱えた、とても貧しい一家に生まれた少年です。チャーリーはチョコレートが大好物ですが、めったに買ってもらえることはありません。それなのに、チャーリーの家のすぐそばには世界一大きくて有名な「ウィリー・ウォンカのチョコレート工場」が立っていて、家の周りにはいつもおいしそうな匂いが漂っています。一度でいいからあの中をのぞいてみたい、チャーリーはいつもそう思っていました。——そんなある日、工場を見学できるという「ゴールデン・チケット」がチョコレートバーの包みに入れられるというニュースが流れ始めます。町は大騒ぎとなり、みんながチョコレートを買いあさりますが、チャーリーが手に入れたチョコは誕生日に買ってもらった一枚だけ。そして、ゴールデン・チケットは全世界でたったの五枚。果たして、チャーリーのチョコの中身は……？

And one was a dark color.

二冊目は生徒と先生のコミカルな戦争を描く、斬新なコメディー『**Frindle**』。予想もしない方向へ展開していく物語と、感動のラストシーンがいつまでも心に残る一作です。

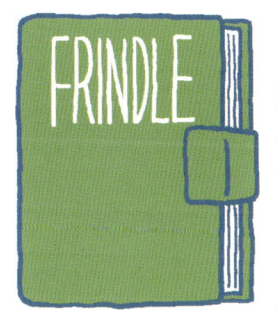

Frindle by Andrew Clements

ニック・アレンは学校の授業を妨害する天才。どんなに退屈な授業も、ニックにかかれば子供たちの思いのまま。そんなニックが新学年にあたったのが、学校一厳しいことで有名なミセス・グランジャーのクラス。「妨害屋」の名にかけて、クラスの期待を一身に背負い、ミセス・グランジャーの宿題をつぶそうとするニックですが、あっけなく見抜かれ、はじめての敗北を味わいます。

このままでは引き下がれないニックは、ある日ミセス・グランジャーが「言葉は誰でも発明できるもの」と授業中に言ったことをきっかけに、ごくふつうのボールペンを「フリンドル」と呼び始めます。辞書を崇拝する国語教師のミセス・グランジャーはそれを厳しく叱りますが、やがてクラス全員がペンを「フリンドル」と呼び始め、次第にそれは町全体に波及し、ついにはテレビ局がその騒動を嗅ぎつけてきて、やがてニックすら想像できなかった事態に……。

最後の三冊目は時に切なく、時におかしい、一人の天才少女をめぐる物語です。思わず吹き出すようなシーンと、雰囲気たっぷりの叙情感が全編にバランスよくあふれていて、いっぱい笑って、いっぱい泣かせてくれる一作です。

They all meowed and meowed at passing strangers — all except for the dark kitten.

Please take me home

Someday Angeline by Louis Sachar

アンジェリーンはなんでも知っている8歳の天才少女。でも、そのために周りのみんなからはうとまれてしまう存在。ゴミ収集が仕事のアンジェリーンのお父さんは、頭の悪い自分から、なぜこんな女の子が生まれたのか分からず、アンジェリーンの将来をだめにしてしまうのではないかと怖がって、ついつい娘と距離を置いてしまいます。アンジェリーンのたったひとつの願いはお父さんとふつうに、幸せに暮らすこと。でも、アンジェリーンの天才的な頭脳でさえ、その願いだけはどうしたらかなうのか分かりません。——そんなアンジェリーンにはじめてできた友達がお調子者のグーン。いつもふざけてばかりいるグーンは、クラスのみんなからもバカにされているおちこぼれの男の子。でも、グーンだけは、アンジェリーンが頭がいいことをまったく気にしませんでした。やがてアンジェリーンを理解する先生も現れて、すべてがうまくいくかに思えた時、運命の歯車が狂い始めて……。

三つのあらすじを読み終わって、気に入ったものはありましたか？　どれも決して簡単ではありませんが、文章そのものは読みやすく、物語や登場人物もなじみやすい作品ばかりです。まずはこの中から一冊を選んでみてください。どうしてもあらすじだけでは決められないという方は、次のチャートへ！

They were all hungry, so they cried and cried.

Big Fat Cat and the Fortune Cookie

「基本の三冊」ヘルプ・チャート

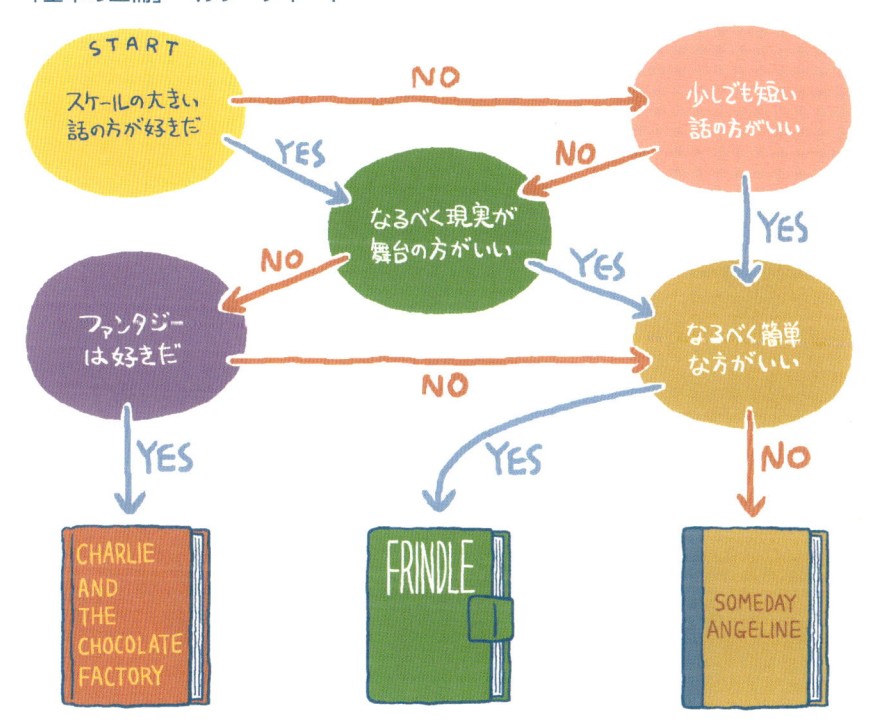

START
スケールの大きい話の方が好きだ → NO → 少しでも短い話の方がいい
↓ YES ↓ YES
なるべく現実が舞台の方がいい ← NO
↓ NO / ↓ YES / YES ↑
ファンタジーは好きだ ← NO → なるべく簡単な方がいい
↓ YES ↓ YES ↓ NO
CHARLIE AND THE CHOCOLATE FACTORY / FRINDLE / SOMEDAY ANGELINE

　ふつうの洋書には **BFC BOOKS** のようなルビも三色辞典もありません。あらすじを読み終えても「自分に読めるだろうか」と不安を感じている方も多いと思います。緊張していると読めるものも読めなくなってしまうので、そういう時は無理をせず、さらに読みやすい一冊を選んでみることをおすすめします。

　たとえば、こんな一冊はいかがですか？

And one by one, they were taken home. First, the two white ones, then, the two striped ones.

Please take me home

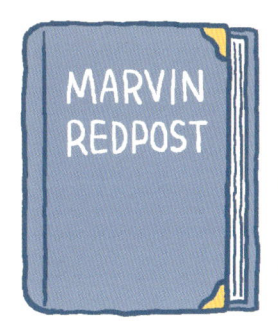

Marvin Redpost: Kidnapped at Birth?
by Louis Sachar

　マービン・レッドポストはどこにでもいる小学生の男の子。ある日、新聞でシャンプーン国の国王が赤ん坊の頃に誘拐された自分の息子を探す記事を見て、ある疑惑を抱きます。自分と特徴が似すぎている！　でもそんなはずはない……頭では分かっていても、マービンは気になって仕方がありません。やがて疑惑は深まっていき、マービンはとんでもない行動を……。

　この本は「基本の三冊」の一冊として紹介した『**Someday Angeline**』の作者による、ライトなコメディーです。文章は『ビッグ・ファット・キャットとマスタード・パイ』ぐらいの難易度なので、若干難しい単語も出てきますが、厄介な表現や言い回しは登場しません。

　三冊＋一冊のうち、どれでもかまいません。──どれか一冊を選んだら、先のページへお進みください。

The kittens left in the box meowed sadly, except the dark one that just yawned.

STEP 2
～ 本を手に入れる ～

　さて、読みたい本は決まりました。でも、まだ大きな問題が残っています。どうやってその本を手に入れるかです。日本では洋書を置いている本屋さんは少ないので、これは意外に大きな難関です。

　現在、日本国内で洋書を手に入れる方法は大きく分けて二つあります。ひとつは書店で注文する方法、もうひとつはインターネットのお店から買う方法です。パソコンを持っていて、インターネットを使ったことのある方なら、一番早く洋書を手に入れられるのは後者です。早いもので数日、遅いものでも一カ月前後で手元に届きます。値段もアメリカで買うのと大差なく、ペーパーバックならほとんどが数百円です。

　もしインターネットのお店を利用するなら、一番有名なのが **amazon** というお店です。各国に支店があって、日本の **amazon** は **amazon.co.jp** と呼ばれています。お店の名前がそのままインターネットのアドレスにもなっていますので、パソコンのブラウザ（インターネットを見るためのソフト）から **http://www.amazon.co.jp** と入力すれば **amazon** につながります。もちろん説明はすべて日本語なので、安心してのぞいてみてください。

　パソコン、インターネットと聞くと、それだけで不安を感じる方もいると思います。もし周りに詳しい人がいたら、家族や友人にお願いして本を買ってもらうのも手です。しかし、英語を学んでいく上でインターネットは強い味方になりますので、できればこれを機にパソコンを使ってみてください。パソコンにはいろいろな機能がありますが、イン

One of the spotted kittens was weak.
It could only purr.
Everyone thought it was sick,
so they never picked it.

Please take me home

ターネットの使い方だけでも覚えておくと、無料で利用できる英和辞典など、役立つ用途がいろいろ見つかるはずです。難しいイメージがあるかもしれませんが、ぜひ一度チャレンジしてみてください。

　少し時間がかかってもいいから、まずは気軽に洋書を手に入れたいという方には、もうひとつの方法がおすすめです。

　幸運なことに、日本ではほとんどの書店から、本のタイトルと作者名、そして **ISBN番号**（バーコードの横に記載されている各書籍に割り当てられた識別番号）を伝えるだけで、あらゆる洋書を注文できるシステムがあります（必要な情報は巻末に一覧として掲載してありますので、注文の際にはこちらをご利用ください）。書店を通して注文するのはとても簡単で手軽な方法ですが、価格が原価よりも高くなってしまったり、入荷するのに時間がかかってしまったりすることがあります。それさえ気にならなければ、とても便利な方法です。また、主要都市には洋書をたくさんそろえている大型書店もあるので、機会があればそちらも探してみてください。

　このほかに、最近の機種なら、ほとんどの携帯電話からも **amazon.co.jp** で買い物が可能です。「ショッピング」の項目の中に「**amazon.co.jp**」が入っていますので、携帯電話に慣れている方は、こちらも便利な選択肢のひとつとして覚えておいてください。

　初めて洋書を手に入れる時はいろいろととまどうこともあると思いますが、その手間は決して学習の妨げにはなりません。重要なステップのひとつです。焦って本を手に入れようとすれば、この作業もイライラするだけの手順になってしまいますが、英語を学ぶ楽しみのひとつだと考えて、何日もかけるつもりでゆっくりやれば、本を手に入れる過程そのものも、その本の思い出の一部となってくれます。そして、思い出がたくさんある本は、心に長く残ります。

　一生大切にするかもしれない本を手に入れるのに、数日を焦っても仕方がありません。ゆっくり、いい思い出を作ってください。

A man took the other spotted kitten. And now there were only two.

Please take me home

STEP 3
~ 本を読む ~

　それぞれ方法はちがうと思いますが、最終的に一冊の本が手元に届くはずです。今回紹介している本のほとんどはペーパーバックという形式で、日本の文庫に当たるものですが、文庫ほど形やフォーマットがはっきり決まっていないので、遊び心のある装丁のものもたくさんあります。持ち運ぶのが楽なように、とても軽くて丈夫な紙でできています。この重さ、手触りがまさに洋書です。読む前にしばらく感触を楽しんでみてください。

　すでにぱらぱらとページをめくってみた方は、思ったよりも分量があって、気が遠くなっているかもしれません。めくっているうちに知らない単語がいくつも目に入ってしまって、不安になっているかもしれません。でも、心配する必要はありません。

　どんな文章でも一行一行ちゃんと読んでいかなければ、ただの記号です。記号がたくさん並んでいるのを見れば、誰でも気が遠くなります。心配するよりも、とりあえず読み始めてみてください。そうすれば、得体の知れない文字列はちゃんとした言葉に変わっていきます。難しいかどうかを判断するのはそれからでも遅くありません。

　辞書は引いても引かなくてもかまいません。ルビをふるのも自由です。自分で色分けをするのもひとつの方法です。寝転んで読んでもいいし、お菓子を食べながら読んでもかまいません。やってはいけないことなんて何ひとつありません。一番楽しい方法で読んでみてください。

> Along came a little girl. She reached inside the box. The weak kitten purred as loud as it could.

読んでいる途中、覚えておいてほしいことがいくつかあります。英語のセリフにはどうしてもスラング（しゃべり言葉ならではの造語）というのが出てきます。スラングはアメリカ人でも全部を理解できるわけではないので、ある程度想像で読みとるのが基本となりますが、どうしても不安な方はスラング辞典を用意するのもいいかもしれません。でも、辞書の類を使うのはできるだけ避けてください。もし辞書を使っていて疲れてきたら、思い切って辞書を部屋の端へ放り投げ、あとは想像で穴埋めをしながら読んでみてください。よく使う表現なら必ず何度も出てきます。出てくるたびに少しずつ正しい意味が分かってきます。そして、たくさん出てこないものなら、特に覚える必要はありません。だから、どうか気にせず読み続けてください。

　ただひとつ大切なこと——それは「難しすぎる」という結論を、あまり急いで出さないことです。

　「難しさ」にも、いろんな種類があります。単純に文章が難解な場合もあれば、作者の個性や特徴で難しく感じてしまう場合もあります。外国語だとついつい語学力のためだと思い込んでしまいがちですが、読み続けることによって難易度が落ちてくる場合もよくあります。これはどんな作者でも、文章のパターンや単語に限りがあるからです。慣れてくると、ちょっと難しい文章でもすらすら読める、なんてこともありますので、難しいからといってすぐにあきらめず、1ページでも多く読んでみてください。

　焦って結論を出さない方がいい理由はほかにもあります。これは児童書に限ったことではありませんが、長い物語の場合、ある程度本の内容に引き込まれて集中するまでは、文章が頭の中へ入ってきません。

　いい物語はその辺も心得ていて、最初の方が頭に入っていなくても支障がないように工夫してあります。だから「よく分からなかったな」と思っても、かまわず進んでください。それは英語が読めなかったからではなくて、意識がまだ物語に入っていない可能性が高いからです。二周目に読み返したら、おどろくほどよく入ってきます。

But the girl reached for the dark kitten. The weak kitten kept purring helplessly.

Please take me home

本を一冊読み切れば、その作者のほかの作品の難易度がぐんと落ちます。さらにその作者の作品をだいたい全部読み尽くせば、その作者が書いているジャンル自体の難易度が落ちます。そして、そのジャンルの主立った本を読み尽くした頃、その言語全体のパターンがつかめてきて、読めない本が少なくなってきます。

　基本はあくまで楽しんで読むことです。何度挫折してもかまいません。だから「少しでも速く読もう」とか、「単語をたくさん覚えよう」とは思わず、目の前にある物語を楽しんでください。

　分からない単語も、文も、たくさん出てくるはずです。でも、いいんです。分からなくても面白いように書かれているのが児童書なのですから。

　ロアルド・ダールが『Matilda』という作品の中で、本を読み始めたばかりの主人公に、こう語りかけています。

　「分からない部分に関しては気にしなくてもいいから。リラックスして、文字が自分の周りを流れていくのを楽しみなさい。音楽を聴くみたいにね」

The dark kitten opened one
eye and scratched
the girl's hand.

Please take me home

STEP 4
〜 本を読み終えたら 〜

　さあ、いよいよ最後のステップです。
　最初に読んだ一冊が最高に面白い本だったとしたら、それに勝ることはありません。でも、もしそうでなかったら──いえ、たとえそうだったとしても、さらにいい本を探し続けたいと思われることでしょう。「基本の三冊」のほかの二冊や、『Marvin Redpost』を読むのももちろんおすすめですが、読み終わった本が面白かったという方には朗報があります。
　実は今回紹介した本はほとんどがシリーズものの始まりの一冊です。もし読んだ一冊が面白かったら、同じキャラクターや、同じ舞台が登場する作品がたくさんあります。シリーズもののいいところは、読み続けることで本当に親しい友人を得るような感覚ができることです。そんな友人の話だったら、英語でも決して苦になりません。
　次のページから、読み終わった本ごとの選択肢を用意しました。これを参考に、どんどん範囲を広げていってください。「基本の三冊」を全部読み終われば、だいぶ選べる範囲は広くなっているはずです。あとは気の向くまま、好きな世界を楽しんでください。

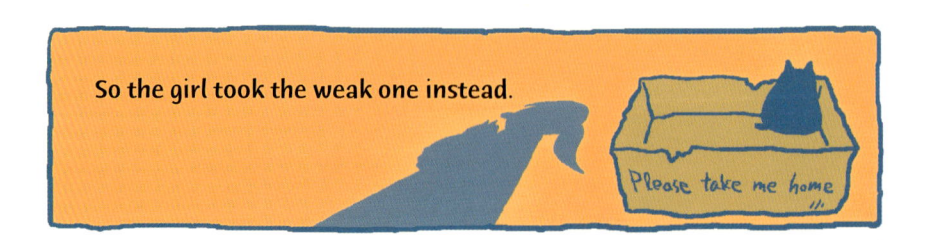

So the girl took the weak one instead.

Please take me home

● ロアルド・ダールの Charlie and the Chocolate Factory を読み終えた方へ

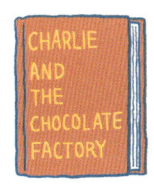

1. Charlie and the Great Glass Elevator（直接の続編）
2. その他のダールの長編作品
3. ダールの短編作品
4. ルイス・サッカーの本（82 ページ参照）

『Charlie and the Chocolate Factory』を面白いと感じた方は幸運です。この物語の作者、ロアルド・ダールは世界でもっとも有名な児童書作家の一人で、素晴らしい作品を数多く残しています。直接の続編である『Charlie and the Great Glass Elevator』という作品も、それ以外の作品も、どれもすばらしいものばかりです。

数ある長編の中でもおすすめなのは、少女マチルダが意地悪な親や先生と戦う『Matilda』や、巨人と女の子の冒険の物語『The BFG』、巨大な桃に乗って虫たちと共に旅をする男の子を描いたダークファンタジー『James and the Giant Peach』などです。

一方、『Chocolate Factory』は面白かったけれど、少し長すぎた、という方には短編の作品もおすすめです。どれも長編の三分の一から五分の一ぐらいの長さで、読むのも苦になりません。おすすめはとびきりシャイなおじいさんが 99 匹の亀を使って、憧れの女性に恋を打ち明ける奇想天外なラブストーリー『Esio Trot』、かなりダークな笑いを満載したブラックユーモアの傑作『George's Marvelous Medicine』、そしてディズニーのアニメ映画を彷彿とさせる、知恵者のお父さんギツネが主人公の『Fantastic Mr. Fox』などの作品です。長編も短編も、どれも夢と希望の隙間に、ちょっぴり毒を含んだ作品ばかりなので、油断していると、心をちくっとやられます。

After that, no one came by for a long time.

Please take me home

● **アンドリュー・クレメンツの Frindle を読み終えた方へ**

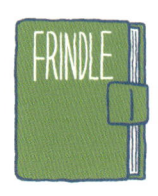

1. その他のクレメンツの作品
2. ルイス・サッカーの本（下記参照）
3. ロアルド・ダールの本（**81** ページ参照）

『Frindle』には残念ながら直接の続編はありません。ただ、作者アンドリュー・クレメンツは似たタイプの物語をたくさん書いています。どれも『Frindle』のニックのような少し変わった少年少女が主人公で、多くの作品は興味のわくグッズやアイテムを中心に展開します。おすすめはパソコンと発想力を駆使して、究極の学級新聞を作る子供たちの物語『The Landry News』、父親が学校の用務員であることを恥じている男の子の物語『The Janitor's Boy』、そして同じクラスの友達が書いた小説を大人のエージェントになりすまして出版しようと試みる小学生の物語『The School Story』です。

クレメンツの物語は小学校を舞台にしたものが多いので、異なる雰囲気のものが読みたければ、ルイス・サッカーやロアルド・ダールの本にも手を出してみてください。『Frindle』を気に入った方なら、きっとどちらも好みに合うと思います。

● **ルイス・サッカーの Someday Angeline を読み終えた方へ**

1. Dogs Don't Tell Jokes（直接の続編）
2. その他のサッカーの長編作品
3. 同作者の Wayside School シリーズ
4. 同作者の Marvin Redpost シリーズ

> Finally when it was night, the dark kitten woke up and realized it was starving. It stretched and looked around.
>
> Please take me home

『Someday Angeline』の作者ルイス・サッカーは今、全米でもっとも人気のある児童書作家の一人です。彼は近年、権威ある児童文学賞二つを同時に受賞するという、史上初の快挙を成し遂げた作家です。その受賞作が邦訳でもヒットとなった『Holes（邦題・穴）』です。『Holes』は大変おすすめの作品ですが、サッカーの本の中ではかなり難易度が高い作品なので、じっくり挑んでほしい一冊です（あらすじは 88 ページ参照）。それ以外の作品も、現代的なストーリーと、生き生きとしたキャラクター、そして鮮やかなラストで、きっと読者の誰もを満足させてくれるはずです。

『Someday Angeline』には、登場人物のその後を追った『Dogs Don't Tell Jokes』という姉妹編が出ています。こちらは『Someday Angeline』に登場したお調子者の少年グーンが、アンジェリーンの励ましを得て、「人を笑わせること」の本当の意味に目覚めていく物語です。学園祭でのタレントコンクールにエントリーしたグーンは、いっしょうけんめい「ウケる」ことを考えているうちに、だんだん自分の内面と向き合っていくことになります。さまざまな人の思惑が絡んで、ラストのコンクール本番は手に汗を握るサスペンスとどんでん返しの連続です。「ジョーク」がテーマの作品だけに、途中分かりにくい場面もあるかと思いますが、かなりのセリフを読みとばす覚悟ででも、ぜひ最後までたどり着いてほしい一冊です。最後の最後でグーンがすべてを懸けて放つ「秘密兵器」は万国共通の笑いなので、ご安心ください。

長い本が苦手な方は同作者の『Wayside School』シリーズがおすすめです。2 ～ 3 ページ程度のショートショートからなるこのシリーズは、どの話も最後にちゃんとオチがついていて、読者を飽きさせません。しかも、シリーズ全体を通しての仕掛けも隠されています。74 ページで紹介した『Marvin Redpost』もサッカーの手によるシリーズです。こちらは『Someday Angeline』よりもずっと読みやすくできています。何巻もまとめて読んでみたい方なら、こちらもおすすめです。

And then, tore open the box.

Please take me home

●ルイス・サッカーの Marvin Redpost を読み終えた方へ

1. Marvin Redpost シリーズを読み続ける
2. 同作者の Wayside School シリーズ
3. ほかのサッカーの作品を読む

　『Marvin Redpost』は実は一冊だけでは本当の面白さが分からないシリーズです。二冊目以降、どんどん面白くなってくるので、ぜひ読み続けてみてください。巻を重ねるごとに登場人物が揃ってきて、やがて全編を通した展開も登場し、世界がどんどん広がっていきます。全部読み終えたらきっと一生忘れられないシリーズになるはずです。
　『Marvin Redpost』では手応えが足りないと感じた方は「基本の三冊」へ戻ってみるか、Marvin シリーズの作者であるルイス・サッカーが書いた別の本を選んでみてください（82 ページ「Someday Angeline を読み終えた方へ」の項目を参照）。

　図にこそ書いてありませんが、読み終えた本がどれであっても、もうひとつ重要な選択肢があります。それは同じ本をもう一度「読み返す」ことです。最後まで話を知っている本を読み返すのはつまらないように感じられますが、二度目こそ本当に面白い読書体験になるはずです。先がどうなるのか知っているからこそ味わい深くなるキャラクターのセリフや行動、一回目には気がつかなかった伏線など、物語を把握してからでないと見えてこない楽しみがいっぱい隠されています。気に入った本はぜひ読み返してみてください。好きなシーンだけでもかまいません。
　もし「基本の三冊」の中から選んだ本が難しく感じられて、どうしても途中で先に進めなくなってしまった方は、ほかの二冊にも目を通してみることをおすすめします。「難

And no one knows
where that kitten is today.

END
Please take me home

易度が同じぐらいなら結果も同じではないのか」と思うかもしれません。確かにその可能性もありますが、本の読みやすさは難易度だけでなく、相性にも大きく左右されています。「基本の三冊」はそれぞれ微妙に傾向のちがう物語で、文体にもだいぶ差があります。『Someday Angeline』が厳しいという方も、『Frindle』ならだいじょうぶということも十分に考えられます。

　もしほかの二冊も今ひとつ入り込めなければ、『Marvin Redpost』をぜひ試してみてください。セリフ部分はスラングが入るので多少厄介ですが、それを除けばとても読みやすい作品です。

　『Marvin Redpost』でも少しぴんとこなかったという方には、さらにとっておきの二作を紹介しておきましょう。これはどちらもかなり読みやすい文章で書かれていますが、同時にとてもひねりの効いた傑作です。

Nate the Great by Marjorie Weinman Sharmat

　この作品はトレンチコートをまとった小学生、ネート・ザ・グレートが渋いナレーションと共に、身近で起こる様々な事件に挑むミステリーのシリーズです。事件はどれも「ものをなくした」とか、「ペットが行方不明になった」とか、一見他愛もないものなのですが、ネートが繰り広げるのはいつも本格的な捜査で、しかもその語り口調はハードボイルドな雰囲気たっぷりです。愛犬スラッジと共に今日もトレンチコートに身を包み、パンケーキをむさぼりながら捜査を続けるネートの活躍をぜひ一度楽しんでみてください。

Amelia Bedelia by Peggy Parish

　この作品は英語の言い回しを覚えるのにもってこいの内容になっています。というのも、主人公であるメイドのアメリアは、どんな言葉もそのままに受け取ってしまう純粋

な女性です。その上、雇い主の頼みはなんでも忠実に実行するので、毎回とんでもない騒ぎを起こしてしまいます。たとえば「**dress the chicken**」というのは「チキンの下ごしらえをする」という言い回しですが、そのままとれば「チキンに服を着せる」という意味になってしまいます。だからアメリアがそれを聞くと……どうなるか分かりますよね。とにかく爆笑させてくれる作品ですが、最後にはちょっと心温まるシーンも用意されています。

『**Nate the Great**』も『**Amelia Bedelia**』もそれぞれ続編が無数に出ている人気シリーズです。この二つのシリーズはどの話から読み始めてもいいようになっていますが、できるだけ最初から読むことをおすすめします。

『**Nate the Great**』を読み終わって、もっとミステリーが読みたいと思った方は『**Encyclopedia Brown**』や『**A to Z Mysteries**』のシリーズもおすすめです。前者はショートショートのミステリーを集めたもので、後者は中編ぐらいの長さの読みやすいシリーズです（詳細は **92** ページに収録してあります）。

どの方向へ向かってもかまいません。どうか自由に児童書の世界を歩いてみてください。

THE NEXT STEP
~ 本をもっと探す ~

　ステップはこれですべて終了です。今まで紹介してきた作品の中に気に入ってもらえるものがあったことを祈っていますが、たとえ見つからなかったとしても、どうかあきらめずに探し続けてください。ここで紹介した物語は数百、数千、数万ある児童書の中のほんの数冊です。しかもなるべく普遍的な、くせのない作品を中心に選んだものばかりです。もっと不気味なものも、シュールなものも、ロマンチックなものも、児童書は限りない広がりを持っています。

　最後にスペースの許す限り、そんないろいろな種類の作品を少しでも紹介していきたいと思います。

Goosebumps by R. L. Stine

　ホラーのジャンルでも児童書は多くの名作を輩出しています。近年このジャンルの代表的な作家といえば、**R. L.** スタインの名前が最初にあがってきます。大ヒットシリーズ『**Goosebumps**』(「鳥肌」の意) は毎回どきっとさせられるオチのついたライトタッチのホラーシリーズで、現在まで 80 冊以上が刊行されています。1 冊読み切りで、幽霊屋敷から **UFO** まであらゆるホラーのジャンルをカバーしているので、各巻のタイトルから、好みに合いそうなものを選んでみてください。どれか一冊を買えば、全作品のリストが載っているはずです。この作者はほかにもいろんなホラーのシリーズを出していますので、そちらも試してみてください。

Holes by Louis Sachar

　すでにおなじみのルイス・サッカーの代表作です。主人公スタンリー・イェルナッツは犯した覚えのない罪のために、青少年矯正施設「グリーン湖キャンプ場」へ送られてしまいます。キャンプ場での生活ならそれほど辛くはないだろうと考えていたスタンリーですが、「グリーン湖」には湖なんてありませんでした。水は何十年も前に干上がり、灼熱の砂漠と化した大地だけがどこまでも広がる恐ろしい場所、それが「グリーン湖キャンプ場」──そこに集められた少年たちは人格矯正の名の元に、毎日大きな穴をひとつずつ地面に掘ることを命じられます。しかし、穴を掘る理由はどうやら矯正ばかりではないようで……。

Ink Drinker by Eric Sanvoisin

　こちらはフランス生まれのダークでおしゃれなファンタジーシリーズです。主人公は本が大嫌いなのに、夏休みの間、お父さんの経営する書店で働くはめになってしまった少年。そこで少年が見かけたのは、なんと懐からストローを取り出して、本の文字を吸っている奇妙な男。あとでその本をめくってみると、ページは真っ白。少年は好奇心から男のあとをつけていきますが……。

Judy Moody by Megan McDonald

　Judy Moody はとても自己顕示欲の強い、気まぐれな女の子。彼女の激しい気分の移り変わりが「グッドムード」「バッドムード」などの言葉であいまいに、そしてポップに表現されています。装丁もセンス良く、そのままインテリアにしてもいいような本です。はちゃめちゃなのに心を打つこの本は、特に女性におすすめの一作です。

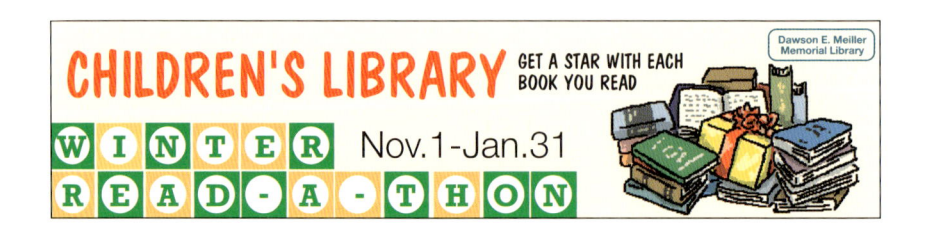

Sammy Keyes by Wendelin Van Draanen

　新感覚の探偵ミステリーシリーズ。ハリウッドの大女優を夢見て出ていってしまった母親を持つ中学生の女の子サミーは、粋なおばあちゃんとの二人暮らし。高齢者専用の福祉アパートに無断で居候しているため、普段はまともに外出もできない生活ですが、持ち前の芯の強さでたくましく日々を生き抜いています。今までの探偵ものとちがうのは、サミー自身には自分が探偵だという自覚がありません。なんとなく事件に巻き込まれ、なんとなく謎を解決してしまいます。第一作はエドガー賞の児童ミステリー部門を受賞しているほどの本格的なミステリーで、謎解きも巧妙で複雑にできています。とても凝った文体で書かれているので、難易度は今回紹介している作品の中でもひときわ高めですが、ミステリーが好きな方なら、きっとこの生意気で魅力的な少女探偵の冒険に心を奪われるはずです。時間をとってじっくり挑戦してみてください。集英社から『少女探偵サミー・キーズ』として翻訳版が発売されているので、最初に日本語で一冊読んで、設定や雰囲気に慣れてから、続きを英語で読んでみるのもひとつの手です。

The Sisterhood of the Traveling Pants by Ann Brashares

　最後に紹介するのは大人気の青春物語。仲良し四人組の少女たちは初めて別々に過ごす夏を記念して、一着の古びたジーンズを交互に履き回すことを誓います。そのジーンズは四人の誰が履いてもぴったりとサイズが合ってしまう不思議なジーンズ。——大人と子供の端境を生きる少女たちが、人生の様々な問題に直面しながらも、互いの友情を支えに成長していく長い夏休みを、一着の奇妙なジーンズを通して描くさわやかな作品です。彼女たちが抱える問題はすべて現実的、現代的で、深刻なものばかりですが、決して暗い作品ではありません。形式としては四人の少女を別々に追っていくので、オムニバス作品に近い形をとっています。難易度は少し高めですが、読み終わればきっと大きな満足感もあるはずです。

魔法の扉を開いて

　BFC BOOKS の制作が始まって以来、おすすめのブックリストを作ろうと、児童書を探し集め、読み続けてきました。しかし、次から次へと面白い本が出てきて、なかなか絞り込むことができず、シリーズもラスト近くになって、やっとこのような形にすることができました。

　あらすじや書評に頼らず、なるべく一冊一冊を読み込んで、本当に面白いと思うものだけを選出したつもりですが、多少偏りがあるかもしれません。──願わくば、今度は自分だけの本のリストを作ってみてください。児童書に関する本も、インターネットのサイトも、たくさんあります。情報を集めて、面白い本をいっぱい見つけて、そして読んでください。

　児童書の世界は果てしなく広い世界です。

　英語はその世界への扉を開く、大切なカギです。

　一旦、そのカギを手に入れたら、いつでも扉を開いて、アメリカの小学校へでも、チョコレートの工場へでも、ドラゴンの棲む魔法の国へでも、好きなだけ出かけていくことができます。指先でページをめくれば、いつでも新しい世界へ旅立つことができます。

　今、そのカギを渡します。

　どうか、たくさんの良い旅を。

Good luck and happy reading!

Big Fat Cat and the Fortune Cookie

THE BIG FAT CAT'S READING LIST

　欧米の出版物は重版や復刻版などの発売時に、出版社や装丁が変わることがよくあります。そのため、一冊の本に何種類ものバージョンがあることも珍しくありません。以下のリストでは基本的にもっとも安価で手に入りやすいアメリカのペーパーバック版を紹介していますが、挿絵などをより美しく楽しみたい方はハードカバー版や豪華本の購入をおすすめします。尚、多くの児童書がオーディオカセットや **CD** 版としても発売されていますので、そちらも参考にしてみてください（巻数の多いシリーズに関しては、最初の五作品だけを掲載しています。また、作者名は共著の場合、片方のみを表記しています）。

※本の表記は著者名／タイトル／総ページ数／ **ISBN** 番号の順に並んでいます。

1. 短くて読みやすい本

Marjorie Weinman Sharmat　***Nate the Great***　64p 044046126X
　シリーズは現在二十四作発売されていて、尚も続刊中。レギュラーの登場人物などは徐々に増えていきますが、基本的に順不同で読むことが可能です。
　Nate the Great Goes Undercover　48p 0440463025
　Nate the Great and the Lost List　48p 0440462827
　Nate the Great and the Phony Clue　48p 0440463009
　Nate the Great and the Sticky Case　48p 0440462894（ほか多数）

Peggy Parish　***Amelia Bedelia***　63p　0064441555
　手書きの綴り字で登場するのが、雇い主の言い付けです。言い回しやたとえなど、どれも二重の取り方ができる文になっています。先を読む前に、その文の本当の意味と、アメリアがそれをどう勘違いするかを想像してから読むと、二倍楽しくなるシリーズです。
　Thank You, Amelia Bedelia　64p 0064441717
　Amelia Bedelia and the Surprise Shower　64p 0064440192
　Come Back, Amelia Bedelia　64p 0064442047
　Play Ball, Amelia Bedelia　64p 0064442055（ほか多数）

2. 言い回しなどが比較的少ない本

Louis Sachar *Marvin Redpost: Kidnapped at Birth?* 68p 0679819460
　何冊も読むことを前提としているシリーズなので、キャラクターが勢ぞろいする二冊目からが本当に面白くなってきます。一作ずつ完結していますが、長い一本の話でもあるのでぜひ順番に。ページ数も少なく、どんどん読めます。
　　Marvin Redpost: Why Pick on Me? 64p 0679819479
　　Marvin Redpost: Is He a Girl? 69p 0679819487
　　Marvin Redpost: Alone in His Teacher's House 83p 0679819495
　　Marvin Redpost: Class President 80p 067988999X （8巻まで）

Eric Sanvoisin *The Ink Drinker* 35p 0440414857
　文章は難しくありませんが、時々変わった単語が出てきます。ほとんど雰囲気を出すためだけに使われているので、ある程度想像で補いながら読みとばしてください。
　　A Straw for Two 48p 0440416655
　　The City of Ink Drinkers 48p 0440418461
　　Little Red Ink Drinker 48p 0440418453 （以下続刊）

Donald J. Sobol *Encyclopedia Brown: Boy Detective* 128p 0553157248
　1960年代に誕生して以来、未だに少年探偵ナンバーワンの座を守っている人気のショートショートシリーズ。各話の最後には読者が謎を解くチャンスが用意されています。
　　Encyclopedia Brown and the Case of the Secret Pitch 128p 0553157361
　　Encyclopedia Brown Finds the Clues 128p 0553157256
　　Encyclopedia Brown Gets His Man 128p 0553157221
　　Encyclopedia Brown Solves Them All 96p 0553480804 （ほか多数）

Ron Roy *The Absent Author (A to Z Mysteries)* 86p 0679881689
　右の一覧を見れば、気がつく方も多いかと思いますが、このシリーズはそれぞれアルファベットの文字をひとつずつ追っています。一冊ずつ完結している作品ですが、探偵役の三人組は全巻共通で登場しています。

The Bald Bandit (A to Z Mysteries) 70p 0679884491
The Canary Caper (A to Z Mysteries) 86p 0679885935
The Deadly Dungeon (A to Z Mysteries) 86p 0679887555
The Empty Envelope (A to Z Mysteries) 78p 0679890548（ほか多数）

3. BFC BOOKS とほぼ同等の難易度の本

Roald Dahl *Charlie and the Chocolate Factory* 155p 0141301155
　途中にイタリックで登場する詩はやや難解なので、とばすことも考慮してください。欧米の児童書にはよく詩が登場しますが、たいていの場合、とばすことが可能です。
　Charlie and the Great Glass Elevator 159p 0141301120

　Esio Trot 62p 0141304642
　序文の **Author's Note** はこの作品に関する作者自身の小話。本編とはあまり関係ありませんが、これだけを読んでも面白いお話です。

　Fantastic Mr. Fox 96p 0141301139
　挿絵が多く、動物が主人公なので、おとぎ話に近い雰囲気です。

　George's Marvelous Medicine 89p 0141301112
　ダールの作品の中でもひときわ読みやすいもので、挿絵が多く、かなりダークな雰囲気です。

　James and the Giant Peach 126p 0140374248
　ティム・バートンがプロデュースした同名の映画がイメージ作りの参考になります（**1996** 年公開作品。邦題『ジャイアント・ピーチ』）。

　The BFG 208p 0141301058
　文章は簡単なのですが、敵の巨人の名前など、造語がたくさん出てくるので注意が必

要です。見たことのないややこしい単語が出てきたら、まず二つ以上の単語をむりやりくっつけた造語であることを疑ってみてください。ちなみに **BFG** はでたらめの文法でしゃべりますが、何を言っているのかはちゃんと分かります。

Matilda 240p 0141301066
ダールの作品ではもっとも長いもののひとつ。物語の冒頭や、多くの章の頭で作者による説明のような部分が入りますが、そこだけはほかよりも難しいので、読みにくければとばしてください。

The Roald Dahl Treasury 448p 067003665X
短編やショートショートを中心に収録した大全集です。ロアルド・ダールの作品をいくつか読んでみて、もし気に入ったなら、この豪華本をおすすめします。上質の用紙にフルカラーで再現されたイラストが本当に美しい一冊です（ただし、長編作品は本編からの抜粋が収録されています）。

The Witches 208p 0141301104
敵役の Grand High Witch はしゃべり方が特徴的で、基本的に w を v として発音し、r は必要以上に強調して rrr と発音することがあります。惑わされないでください。

Louis Sachar *Sideway Stories from Wayside School* 128p 0380698714
Introduction は難しければ、とばすことも可能です。全体に独特のはちゃめちゃなノリの本なので、「読み間違い？」と疑っても、気にせず読み進めてください。すぐに慣れます。

Wayside School is Falling Down 192p 0380754843
Wayside School Gets a Little Stranger 176p 0380723816
Sideways Arithmetic from Wayside School 89p 0590457268
More Sideways Arithmetic from Wayside School 94p 0590477625

Megan McDonald *Judy Moody* 160p 0763612316
Judy 語ともいえる変わった単語がいっぱい出てくるので、あまり気にせず読みとば

The Bald Bandit (A to Z Mysteries) 70p 0679884491
The Canary Caper (A to Z Mysteries) 86p 0679885935
The Deadly Dungeon (A to Z Mysteries) 86p 0679887555
The Empty Envelope (A to Z Mysteries) 78p 0679890548 （ほか多数）

3. BFC BOOKS とほぼ同等の難易度の本

Roald Dahl *Charlie and the Chocolate Factory* 155p 0141301155
　途中にイタリックで登場する詩はやや難解なので、とばすことも考慮してください。欧米の児童書にはよく詩が登場しますが、たいていの場合、とばすことが可能です。
　Charlie and the Great Glass Elevator 159p 0141301120

Esio Trot 62p 0141304642
　序文の **Author's Note** はこの作品に関する作者自身の小話。本編とはあまり関係ありませんが、これだけを読んでも面白いお話です。

Fantastic Mr. Fox 96p 0141301139
　挿絵が多く、動物が主人公なので、おとぎ話に近い雰囲気です。

George's Marvelous Medicine 89p 0141301112
　ダールの作品の中でもひときわ読みやすいもので、挿絵が多く、かなりダークな雰囲気です。

James and the Giant Peach 126p 0140374248
　ティム・バートンがプロデュースした同名の映画がイメージ作りの参考になります（**1996** 年公開作品。邦題『ジャイアント・ピーチ』）。

The BFG 208p 0141301058
　文章は簡単なのですが、敵の巨人の名前など、造語がたくさん出てくるので注意が必

要です。見たことのないややこしい単語が出てきたら、まず二つ以上の単語をむりやりくっつけた造語であることを疑ってみてください。ちなみに **BFG** はでたらめの文法でしゃべりますが、何を言っているのかはちゃんと分かります。

Matilda 240p 0141301066
ダールの作品ではもっとも長いもののひとつ。物語の冒頭や、多くの章の頭で作者による説明のような部分が入りますが、そこだけはほかよりも難しいので、読みにくければとばしてください。

The Roald Dahl Treasury 448p 067003665X
短編やショートショートを中心に収録した大全集です。ロアルド・ダールの作品をいくつか読んでみて、もし気に入ったなら、この豪華本をおすすめします。上質の用紙にフルカラーで再現されたイラストが本当に美しい一冊です（ただし、長編作品は本編からの抜粋が収録されています）。

The Witches 208p 0141301104
敵役の Grand High Witch はしゃべり方が特徴的で、基本的に w を v として発音し、r は必要以上に強調して rrr と発音することがあります。惑わされないでください。

Louis Sachar *Sideway Stories from Wayside School* 128p 0380698714
Introduction は難しければ、とばすことも可能です。全体に独特のはちゃめちゃなノリの本なので、「読み間違い？」と疑っても、気にせず読み進めてください。すぐに慣れます。

- *Wayside School is Falling Down* 192p 0380754843
- *Wayside School Gets a Little Stranger* 176p 0380723816
- *Sideways Arithmetic from Wayside School* 89p 0590457268
- *More Sideways Arithmetic from Wayside School* 94p 0590477625

Megan McDonald *Judy Moody* 160p 0763612316
Judy 語ともいえる変わった単語がいっぱい出てくるので、あまり気にせずに読みとば

す勢いで。現在は四作目まで発売されていて、さらに続刊中。
Judy Moody Gets Famous! 144p 0763619310
Judy Moody Saves the World 96p 0744590507
Judy Moody Predicts the Future 160p 0744583438（以下続刊）

Andrew Clements *Frindle* 105p 0689818769
一部、辞書からの引用などがイタリックで出てくる部分がありますが、そこはわざと難しく書かれています。分からなくても気にしないでください。
The Landry News 138p 0689828683
The School Story 224p 0689851863
The Janitor's Boy 140p 068983585X（ほか多数）

R. L. Stine *Goosebumps: Welcome to Dead House* 144p 0439568471
心霊現象、**UFO**、怪物、サイコサスペンス、ダークファンタジーと、とにかくホラーと名のつくものはこの長いシリーズ中、一度はとり上げられているといっても過言ではありません。一冊一冊読み切りになっていますが、シリーズになっているものもあります。
Goosebumps: Stay Out of the Basement 144p 0439568455
Goosebumps: Monster Blood 144p 0439568390
Goosebumps: Say Cheese and Die! 144p 0439568420
Goosebumps: The Curse of the Mummy's Tomb 144p 0439568277（ほか多数）

4. 言い回しなどが比較的多い本

Louis Sachar *Someday Angeline* 160p 0380834448
Dogs Don't Tell Jokes 209p 0679833722
The Boy Who Lost His Face 198p 0679886222
There's a Boy in the Girl's Bathroom 195p 0394805720
最初の二作（特に二作目）には大量のジョークが出てきます。中には英語の特性を使った独特のダジャレも入っているので、しばらく考えて分からなかったら、無視して先

に進んでください。
　あとの二作は特に共通の登場人物などがいるわけではないのですが、『Someday Angeline』『Dogs Don't Tell Jokes』と読後感、雰囲気などが近い作品です。上の二冊を気に入った方ならぜひ。

5. 一般書に近い難易度の本

Louis Sachar ***Holes***　233p　0440414806
　多少難しい作品なので、朗読 CD や映画の DVD、および翻訳本などをうまく使い分けながら読んでみてください。

Wendelin Van Draanen ***Sammy Keyes and the Hotel Thief***　163p　0679892648
　文中に出てくる Grams はサミーのおばあちゃんの愛称。Grandma を縮めたものと思われます。Double Dynamo は主人公たちが大好きなアイスクリームの名前。登場するキャラクターの名前がかなり個性的なので、登場人物表を作りながら読んだ方が、後半の謎解きが分かりやすいかもしれません。
　Sammy Keyes and the Skeleton Man　224p　0439981247
　Sammy Keyes and the Sisters of Mercy　210p　0375801839
　Sammy Keyes and the Runaway Elf　186p　037580255X
　Sammy Keyes and the Curse of Moustache Mary　256p　0440416434（ほか多数・続刊中）

Ann Brashares ***The Sisterhood of the Traveling Pants***　294p　0385730586
　プロローグだけがほかよりも少し難しいので、手こずった場合、かまわないのでとばしてしまってください。ちゃんと話は通じます。二周目に読み返す時ならきっとプロローグも読みやすくなっているはずです。
　The Second Summer of the Sisterhood　384p　0552550507

TIPS FROM THE CAT
A DAY IN SCHOOL

児童文学の作品の多くは、小学校や
その周辺部を舞台にしています。
高校や大学の様子は映画などでもよく登場しますが、
小学校というのはめったに出てこないので、
なかなか想像しにくい場所になっています。
そこで、今回の **TIPS FROM THE CAT** では、
アメリカの小学校にしばし体験入学をしていただきます。
きっと児童書を読む時の参考になるはずです。

WELCOME TO GRADE SCHOOL

PLAYGROUND
運動場はたいてい日本の小学校よりも小さめで、芝生が敷き詰められていることが多い。週に数回は中央の国旗掲揚台の前に全校生徒が集まって、胸に手を当ててみんなで「Pledge of Allegiance to the Flag（国旗に対する忠誠の誓い）」を復唱する。
体育の授業は主にバスケットボールやバレーボールなどの球技を中心に行われ、子供が競争心やチームワークを養うことに重点が置かれている。

FENCE
周囲は安全のために、頑丈な垣根などでぐるり一周閉ざされている。

CLASSROOMS 1
一階の玄関近くには低学年の教室がある。低学年のうちは比較的規律が厳しく、机もきちんと並べられているのが一般的。高学年になるに従って、生徒の自由に任せていく。

BULLETIN BOARD
目につきやすい場所に掲示板があって、毎朝登校時に目を通すことになっている。

ENTRANCE
登下校時には、道路沿いに親の迎えの車が一列に並んで待っている。誘拐などを防ぐために、先生が親の顔を確認してから子供を乗車させる。玄関先に必ずベンチがたくさんあるのは、迎えが来るまで子供達がここで待つため。
自宅から学校まで何キロもある地方では、スクールバスや親の車による登校が多い。都市部などでは徒歩や自転車の通学も見られる。

日本では小学校の教育方針は国が主導権を握っていますが、アメリカでは町や市などの地方自治体が管理しています。このため、地域によって極めて大きな貧富の差があり、設備や環境などが学校ごとに著しくちがっています。もっとも貧しい地域では、紙やペンといった文房具もままならず、定期的に担任の先生が自ら生徒に買い与えているのが現状です（このための特別減税制度があるほどです）。今回紹介している小学校は中級から上級クラスの小学校で、平均的な環境ですが、あくまで一例に過ぎません。この図ではどこの小学校にでもある最小限の設備しか描いていませんが、多くの学校はこのほかに **Gymnasium**（体育館）、**Science Room**（理科室）、**Music Room**（音楽室）などを持っています。

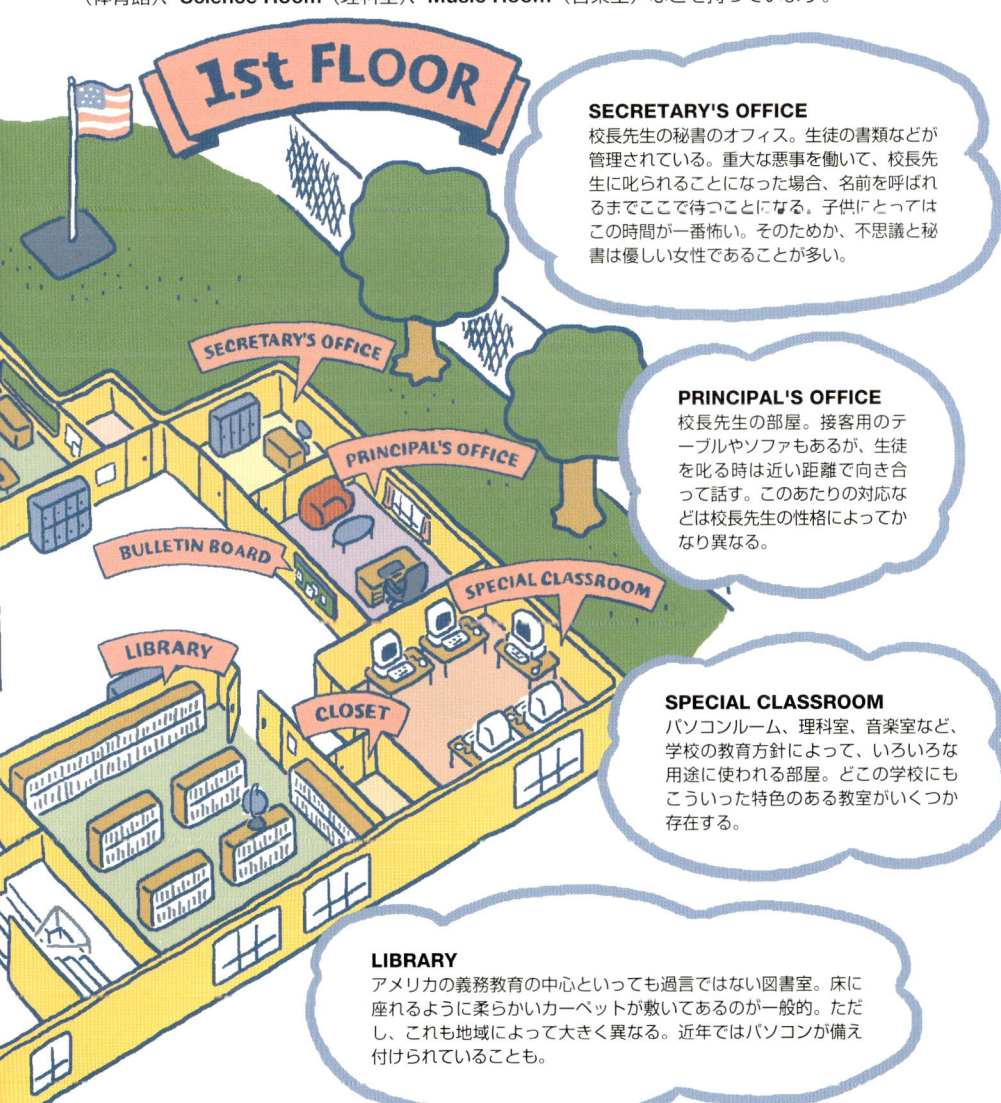

1st FLOOR

SECRETARY'S OFFICE
校長先生の秘書のオフィス。生徒の書類などが管理されている。重大な悪事を働いて、校長先生に叱られることになった場合、名前を呼ばれるまでここで待つことになる。子供にとってはこの時間が一番怖い。そのためか、不思議と秘書は優しい女性であることが多い。

PRINCIPAL'S OFFICE
校長先生の部屋。接客用のテーブルやソファもあるが、生徒を叱る時は近い距離で向き合って話す。このあたりの対応などは校長先生の性格によってかなり異なる。

SPECIAL CLASSROOM
パソコンルーム、理科室、音楽室など、学校の教育方針によって、いろいろな用途に使われる部屋。どこの学校にもこういった特色のある教室がいくつか存在する。

LIBRARY
アメリカの義務教育の中心といっても過言ではない図書室。床に座れるように柔らかいカーペットが敷いてあるのが一般的。ただし、これも地域によって大きく異なる。近年ではパソコンが備え付けられていることも。

アメリカの小学校ではたいてい明確な時間割が決められていません。各クラスの担任が個別にカリキュラムを組んでいるためです。たとえば机の配列ひとつとっても、厳しい先生のクラスでは日本の小学校のようにきっちり並べられていますが、子供の自主性を重んじる先生のクラスでは、かなり変わった配置になっています。この学校でも高学年の教室では、四年生は机を取り払って、先生を中心に床に座って授業を行い、五年生は机を円状に並べ替えています。六年生に至っては、机の周りにひとつずつ段ボールを貼って壁を作り、それぞれ自分の部屋のように飾りつけています。また、それによってできた通路にも「メインストリート」というように、生徒によってそれぞれ呼び名がつけられています。

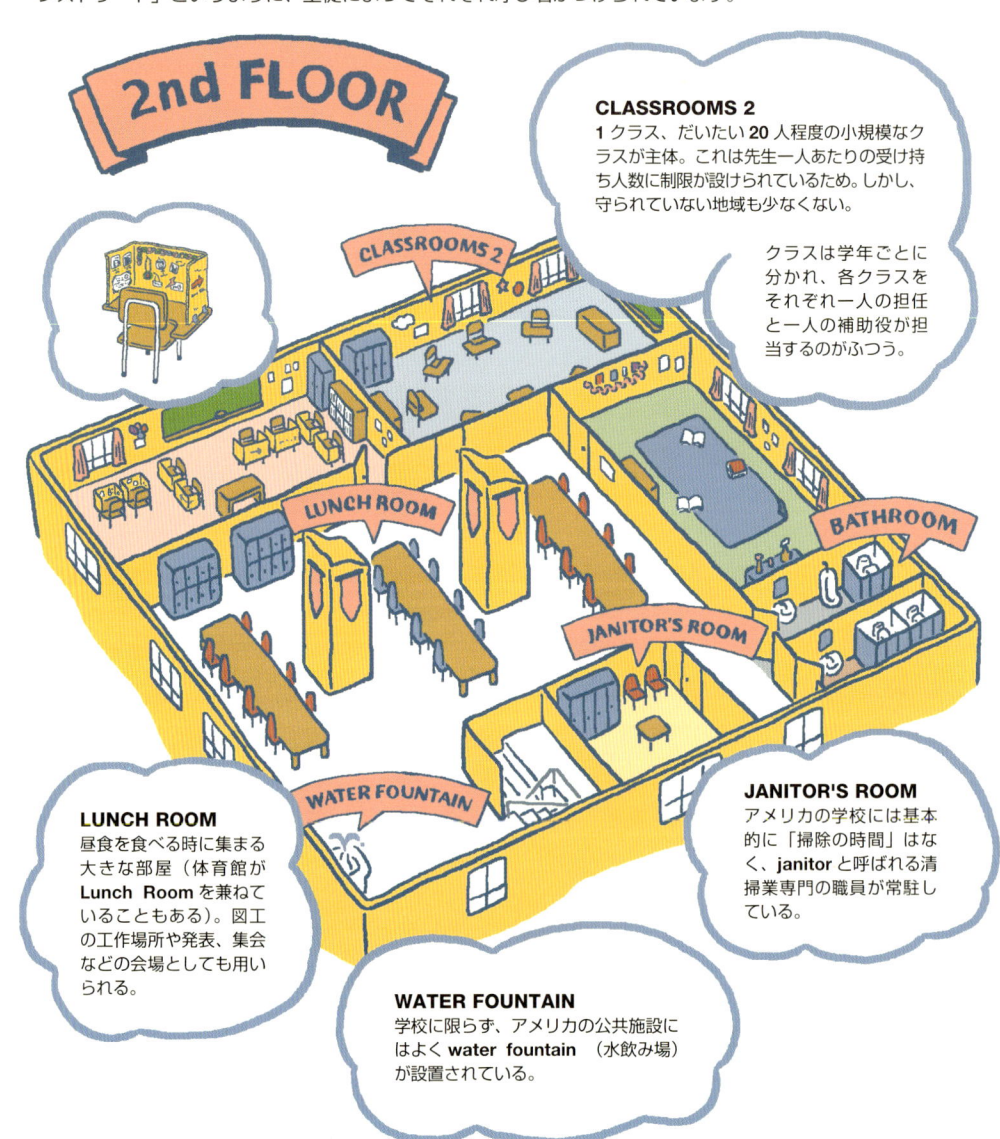

2nd FLOOR

CLASSROOMS 2
1クラス、だいたい20人程度の小規模なクラスが主体。これは先生一人あたりの受け持ち人数に制限が設けられているため。しかし、守られていない地域も少なくない。

クラスは学年ごとに分かれ、各クラスをそれぞれ一人の担任と一人の補助役が担当するのがふつう。

LUNCH ROOM
昼食を食べる時に集まる大きな部屋（体育館がLunch Roomを兼ねていることもある）。図工の工作場所や発表、集会などの会場としても用いられる。

WATER FOUNTAIN
学校に限らず、アメリカの公共施設にはよくwater fountain（水飲み場）が設置されている。

JANITOR'S ROOM
アメリカの学校には基本的に「掃除の時間」はなく、janitorと呼ばれる清掃専門の職員が常駐している。

先生と家庭との連絡はほとんど手書きのメモで行われます。早退する時や、迎えが遅くなる時には、親からのメモを子供が先生に渡し、生徒が悪いことをした時には、先生はその内容をメモに書いて、生徒に持って帰らせます。生徒はそれを親に見せて、確認のサインをもらい、次の日に学校に持ってこなければなりません。

例外もありますが、多くの小学校では教科書は学校から貸し出される形を取っています。アメリカの教科書はたいてい分厚く、毎日持ち帰るようなものではないので、学校の書棚や机の中に置いて帰ります。このため、教科書は落書きだらけになっていたり、破れたりしていて、あまりいい状態とはいえません。

先生はふつう、子供たちを「Ed」というように名前で呼びますが、叱る場合だけは逆に大人扱いして「**Mr. Wishbone**」というように呼び換えます。下の名前で呼ばれると、子供たちがびくっとなるのはこのためです。

LUNCH

ほとんどの小学校では家から昼食を持参するか、あらかじめ学校で **hot lunch** を注文しておきます。一カ月のはじめにメニューが配られる **hot lunch** の中身は、だいたいチキンナゲット、スパゲッティ、ビーフストロガノフ、ターキーサンドイッチなどがメインで、これにニンジンやグリーンピースなどの野菜が一皿と、パイやケーキのようなデザートが付きます。値段は極めて安いのですが、その分、味は期待しない方がいいでしょう。

ラップに包まれたサンドイッチ。一番人気はピーナッツバターとジャム。ハムとチーズ、ツナなどもポピュラーな組み合わせ。

チップスやチョコレートバーが入っていることも多い。

魔法瓶に具だくさんのスープを持参する子も多い。もっとも、缶詰を温めただけのものであることがほとんど。

昼食はたいてい茶色の紙袋か、アニメのキャラクターなどの絵がプリントされたランチボックスに入っている。

追加で飲み物などを買うお金が入っている。**lunch money** と呼ばれる。

『ビッグ・ファット・キャットとフォーチュン・クッキー』の最後に

　BFCシリーズは楽しむための本です。スタッフも編集者も一度として教材と考えたことはありません。だから、読んでいる間、楽しんでもらえたなら、それで十分です。

　でも、このシリーズを振り返って、もしひとつだけ覚えていてほしいことがあるとしたら、それは言葉をしゃべっているのはいつも人間だということです。英語に見えても、日本語に見えても、エドがしゃべっているのも、ジェレミーがしゃべっているのも、いつも彼らの心の中にある気持ちです。出てくる音の種類はたいしたちがいではありません。

　だから、英語が苦手でも、ここまで来た方には彼らの言葉は伝わっていると思います。それは彼らのことを知っていて、彼らの気持ちが分かるからです。言葉を分かるための最大のコツは、勉強でも反復でもありません。「A → B」でも「A = B」でもありません。それは、その言葉をしゃべっている人の気持ちを分かりたいと思うことです。このシリーズで書かれていることはすべて忘れてもらってかまいません。だから、どうかそのことだけは、英語を続けていく上でいつまでも忘れないでください。ここまで付き合ってくださった方々へ、スタッフからの最後のお願いです。

　それでは泣いても笑っても、残ったのはあと一冊です。エドと猫はどこへ行き着くのか？　その結末を知るのにふさわしい日がやってきます。一年に一度だけ奇跡が起こることが許されている日──12月25日、クリスマス。今度雪が降り始めたとき、この物語は終わりを告げます。

　次回、「ビッグ・ファット・キャット・シリーズ」最終回『Big Fat Cat and the Snow of the Century』で、もう一度お会いしましょう！

向山貴彦

　当シリーズは英文法の教科書ではなく、あくまで「英語を読む」ことを最大の目的として作られています。そのため、従来の英文法とはいささか異なる解釈を用いている部分があります。これらの相違は英語に取り組み始めたばかりの方にも親しみやすくするため、あえて取り入れたものです。

STAFF

written and produced by	企画・原作・文・解説	
Takahiko Mukoyama	向山貴彦	
illustrated by	絵・キャラクターデザイン	
Tetsuo Takashima	たかしまてつを	
rewritten by	文章校正	
Tomoko Yoshimi	吉見知子	
art direction by	アートディレクター	
Yoji Takemura	竹村洋司	
DTP by	DTP	
Aya Nakamura	中村文	
technical advice by	テクニカルアドバイザー	
Takako Inoue	井上貴子	
edited by	編集	
Masayasu Ishihara	石原正康（幻冬舎）	
Shoji Nagashima	永島賞二（幻冬舎）	
Atsushi Hino	日野淳（幻冬舎）	
editorial assistance by	編集協力	
Yutaka Inoue	井上裕	
Daisaku Takeda	武田大作	
Kaori Miyayama	宮山香里	
English-language editing by	英文校正	
Michael Keezing	マイクル・キージング（keezing.communications）	
supportive design by	デザイン協力	
Akira Hirakawa	平川彰（幻冬舎デザイン室）	
Miyuki Matsuda	松田美由紀（幻冬舎デザイン室）	
supervised by	監修	
Atsuko Mukoyama	向山淳子（梅光学院大学）	
Yoshihiko Mukoyama	向山義彦（梅光学院大学）	
a studio ETCETERA production	製作 スタジオ・エトセトラ	
published by	発行	
GENTOSHA	幻冬舎	

special thanks to:
Mac & Jessie Gorham　マック＆ジェシー・ゴーハム
Baiko Gakuin University　梅光学院大学

series dedicated to "Fuwa-chan," our one and only special cat

---

BIG FAT CAT オフィシャルウェブサイト
http://www.studioetcetera.com/bigfatcat

幻冬舎ホームページ
http://www.gentosha.co.jp

〈著者紹介〉
向山貴彦　1970年アメリカ・テキサス州生まれ。作家。製作集団スタジオ・エトセトラを創設。デビュー作『童話物語』(幻冬舎文庫)は、ハイ・ファンタジーの傑作として各紙誌から絶賛された。向山淳子氏、たかしまてつを氏との共著『ビッグ・ファット・キャットの世界一簡単な英語の本』は、英語修得のニュー・スタンダードとして注目を浴び、ミリオンセラーとなった。

たかしまてつを　1967年愛知県生まれ。フリーイラストレーターとして、雑誌等で活躍。1999年イタリアのボローニャ国際絵本原画展入選。著書に『ビッグ・ファット・キャットのグリーティング・カード』(幻冬舎文庫)。

ビッグ・ファット・キャットとフォーチュン・クッキー
2004年6月30日　第1刷発行
2016年11月25日　第2刷発行

著　者　　向山貴彦　たかしまてつを
発行者　　見城　徹

発行所　　株式会社 幻冬舎
　　　　　〒151-0051 東京都渋谷区千駄ヶ谷4-9-7

電話:03(5411)6211(編集)
　　 03(5411)6222(営業)
振替:00120-8-767643
印刷・製本所:株式会社 光邦

検印廃止

万一、落丁乱丁のある場合は送料当社負担でお取替致します。小社宛にお送り下さい。本書の一部あるいは全部を無断で複写複製することは、法律で認められた場合を除き、著作権の侵害となります。定価はカバーに表示してあります。

©TAKAHIKO MUKOYAMA, TETSUO TAKASHIMA, GENTOSHA 2004
Printed in Japan
ISBN 4-344-00634-8 C0095

幻冬舎ホームページアドレス　http://www.gentosha.co.jp/

この本に関するご意見・ご感想をメールでお寄せいただく場合は、comment@gentosha.co.jpまで。